Poetry is not my strong suit. Prose is more my style. But Chris Maxwell's book of poems is stimulating and thought-provoking. Take "slow God" for instance.

> after the waiting-on-this-forever action surprises, and 1.
> a slow and sudden God   I consider

Chris gets it and communica... His pace in His timing for our good. While w... wait. It seems slow, "working leisurely," "acting sluggishly." But when the time is right, "many actions seem to happen all at once." Some people are pie-in-sky all the time, faking it I assume. I prefer real. And Chris is real. He tells it like it is. Waiting on God is no fun. It's challenging. Takes "way too long." But God always shows up. He fulfills His promises. Slowly. Yes. And suddenly with just what I need when I need it.

> for us, or at least for me, that is good.
> that is very good.

For me, too. Thanks, Chris, for these poems, comforting yet challenging, deep and simple, and very good!

—Ron White, EdD
president, Emmanuel College

Many people write. Not many write in living color. Thank you, Chris for leaving out no colors, for not shying away from the grays, mudded browns, and even the black tones of this life, yet somehow allowing the ink in your pen to be transformed, sometimes mid-line, into colors of hope, light and resolve because that's what God does with our pens, if we allow Him to.

—Michele Pillar
three time Grammy Award nominated singer,
speaker and author of: *Untangled, The Truth Will Set You Free.*

Chris Maxwell's words have guided me for quite some time. He blends his words beautifully. They paint pictures and unlock imagination. He never uses words to forcefully direct or bully you; his words are the kind of words that breath life and gracefully usher in a new thought or feeling. Even before this latest project, I have always thought of Chris as a poet; a poet of the Davidic type, who's words are raw and untamed, but in them you find your way home. His words have done that for me on many occasions.

Our world needs poets now more than ever. Our sound-bite culture is desperate for a new rhythm—and Chris provides it. This is a book to take your time with, and if you do, you will find these words slipping past your mind and renewing your heart.

—Charlie Dawes
Lead Pastor of Metro Church
Author of *Simple Prayer: Learning to Speak to God with Ease*

The poems in Chris Maxwell's *a slow and sudden God: 40 years of wonder* have the honesty, passion, and insight of David's psalms. Proceeding from decades of ministry and out of years of struggle with epilepsy, Chris's poems combine literariness with accessibility, imagination with gut-level reality, and insights into the contemporary world with poetic responses to, and rewritings of, Biblical texts. His poems are written to draw people to God at the very points of their struggles, and they can be appreciated by anyone from teens to the elderly and everyone in between. If you don't usually read poetry, you will easily relate to Chris's accessible poetry. If you have read poetry for years, you'll appreciate Chris's imagery, originality, and imagination. Chris is a new voice in Christian letters, but his is a voice speaking to everyone.

—Dr. James Rovira
multigenre/multimodal freelance writer, scholar, and poet

Poetry is a way of seeing and processing the world. It sharpens focus and makes one see more clearly in order to record concisely. The sparseness of poetry reveals the depth of struggle and the height of joy, not to mention the discovery of one's reaction to life's circumstances.

In a day of excess verbiage, who would have thought Twitter, with its original limit of 140 characters, could have achieved success. With its demand of making one say more in less words, Twitter's expectation of conciseness caused people to pause, reflect, and think again about what they were trying to communicate.

Chris, in psalm-like quality, has used his poetry to examine his trials, ask his questions, express his frustration, and pour out his praise as a means of processing his trials, which could have ended in defeat . . . but didn't.

—Curt Dalaba
secretary-treasurer,
Michigan District of the Assemblies of God

Reading poetry requires levels of mental attention and heart openness that transcends the usual reading of prose. Like reading the best of Hebrew poetry in the Psalms, Chris Maxwell allows us to join him as he encounters life, love, and God. These contemporary psalms open doors to a world of questions, hopes, dreams, disappointments. They invite us to sit at table with a man moving through life at the speed of hope. Take your time as you read. Ponder. Pause. Pray. Participate.

—Dr. A.D. Beacham, Jr.
general superintendent,
International Pentecostal Holiness Church

When God formed Chris Maxwell, He surely needed a willing vessel in whom to deposit an abundance of gifts, communication not being the least of them. His skill as a master wordsmith shines through in all of his writing, but especially so in this unique collection of free verse. His transparency regarding life issues gives him an instant connection with readers of all ages. Thank you, Chris, for letting us share your joys and struggles.

—Shirley G. Spencer

I have read all Chris's books over the years. But, this one is different. While he still has the capacity to write powerful sentences, paragraphs, and chapters, Chris's poetry caught me off guard. Something about the poetic license, halting abruptness to punctuate a point, fluid lyrical phrases, and playful nature of poetry amplifies and enlarges the power of his thoughts turned into words. I felt like he understood me and knew about my life struggles as he reflects deeply from his own. This is Chris Maxwell at his best! Chris's words bridge the common with the profound. He has the unique ability to turn a phrase, change a letter, or shift an emphasis in such a manner that it feels like someone turned on the lights, and my emotions, feelings, and shared experiences acquired a voice. And his voice resonates with my experience in such a way that you can almost feel the tension between light and dark, sweet and bitter, sin and redemption. I love Chris's books, but this one is my favorite.

—C. Tracy Reynolds
vice-president for student development
dean, School of Christian Ministries
Emmanuel College

Chris Maxwell loves words. He turns to words to make sense of his life's pain and to search for a compassionate, amazing God. The pairing of hard times and radiant hope means he makes much of the word yet. As in this early poem:

> i am needy and alone,
> yet, i am complete and never forsaken.

What a remarkable and eloquent capturing of our human condition and Christ's provision.

Later, acknowledging the infirmity of illness and weight of uncertainty, he pivots once again: "yet, i will sing through the pain." And sing Chris does, with lines that ring with all kinds of possibilities for we who are privileged to read Chris's words.

—Timothy Jones
dean of Trinity Episcopal Cathedral
and author of *The Art of Prayer* and *Awake My Soul*

Chris Maxwell is a wordsmith, or better yet, a word magician. He understands the latent power of words, and is adept at arranging them in contrasts and complements so as to release their hidden potency. His word-spells radiate shafts of beauty and grace that illuminate the drabness of everyday life. These poetic incantations do not induce drowsiness, but rather awaken us to the glory that suffuses every day that the Lord has made.

—Russell Board
regional director for Continental Asia,
IPHC World Missions Ministries

When I read poetry from Chris Maxwell, he reminds me what a precious, miraculous, and powerful thing are words, and what a gift is life. Chris, too, is a gift.

—Craig Brian Larson,
pastor and author of the Kindle eBook
Hang in There to the Better End

I first met Chris Maxwell through my book, *Sacred Pauses*, and his book, *Pause: The Secret to a Better Life One Word at a Time*. Along with the common ground of our two books, I became inspired by his personal story—how he met a devastating health diagnosis with faith and honest struggle, and continued to persevere in the midst of challenge. His life and work are a testimony to God's grace.

Chris writes with clarity and from the heart. His prose has always seemed like poetry to me, and I'm glad that his poetic voice comes to the forefront in this new collection. I love the wide embrace of the title, *a slow and sudden God*, and for the way his poems make room for words that "fit" and words that "fall apart," for questions of call and response, for thinking and feeling, and the wide expanse of human experience. His poetry is both personal reflection and deeply theological—for heart, soul, and mind. Thank you, Chris, for sharing your poems and your life.

—April Yamasaki
pastor and author of
Sacred Pauses: Spiritual Practices for Personal Renewal,
Upside-Down Living: Sharing Faith Stories,
Four Gifts: Seeking Self-Care for Heart, Soul, Mind, and Strength,
and other books on Christian living

Rachel,
Rest in the moments.

a slow and sudden God

40 years of wonder

Psalm 19

Chris Maxwell

True Potential
REACH THE WORLD

a slow and sudden God
40 years of wonder
by Chris Maxwell

© 2018 by Chris Maxwell

ISBN: 978-1-948794-20-6 (paperback)
ISBN: 978-1-948794-21-3 (eBook)

Library of Congress Control Number: 2018951079

Printed in the United States of America.

This book is dedicated to Nathan Dana Taylor

Contents

acknowledgments

Breakfast. I'm imagining breakfast.

The aroma of scrambled eggs, coffee for you and juice for me, and strawberry jelly for my lightly toasted wheat toast.

The noise of conversations of generations. Family members who love words spoken, written. Words into music to be played and sang. Stories to be told. Laughter to be enjoyed. Time to be valued.

Time with food and words. Time together.

Who is there in this imagined kitchen as the fan whirls and the birds sing outside the open windows? A few of the many I need to thank. I imagine this time of grinning at them as I say thank you.

A thank you to Nathan Dana Taylor, my great grandfather who was a poet and a musician. I'm grateful I spent my first few years knowing him. Papa Taylor wrote:

Think on These Things[1]
Phil. 4:8

As we read the words of scripture,
   See the pleasant word it brings
'Whatsoever things are lovely'
   We should look upon these things . . .

Lovely scenes are all about us,
   God has made our world this way,
Now He tells us to behold them,
   Think upon them day by day.

Gorgeous colors, gold and purple
   Slowly fading in the west,
Passing Splendor of the sunset,
   Nature—lying down to rest.

---

1   Nathan Dana Taylor, *Sunset and Morning* (New York: Pageant Press. Inc., 1959) 28–29.

A thank you to Carolyn Acker Maxwell, my mother who told amazing stories and wrote kind words. I'm thankful I spent my first nineteen years knowing her. I found this poem as I was going through Mama's writing. She may have written it (we couldn't find an author), but if she didn't write the poem, she thought it important enough to write it in her journal. It represents the kind and loving person she was.

Words

They are such tiny little things
The words we say each day.
And yet they make for someone
The world seem dull or gay.

The little words of gossip
That we unthinking said
Left someone hurt and wounded
With hope all crushed and dead.

The little word of kindness,
Made all the world a song,
And someone found the journey
Less weary and less long.

So as we go along our way,
Whate'er the way may be,
Let's speak a word of love and cheer
To everyone we see.

A thank you to my father and sisters, to all my relatives and friends. A thank you to poets and artists and storytellers. A thank you to those who've welcomed my style and encouraged me to continue writing. A thank you to high school and college English professors—Phyllis Synan and Joyce Taylor—who read my writing and challenged me to continue. A thank you to all who accepted me and my damaged brain—your willingness to enjoy breakfast with me has been fitting and needed therapy. A thank you to James Rovira, Paul W. Smith, and Steve Spillman—our conversations and your changes in this book helped make the meal a better breakfast for all.

A thank you to the Poet who knows all about me, and still sits beside me at this life meal—in the beginning was the Word.

A thank you to my wife Debbie, who has traveled with me through so many of these poetic decades.

A thank you to our sons—Taylor, Aaron, Graham—and their wives and children. Each of them bring poetic rhythm to our lives, even from a distance.

Since we included some poetic thoughts from generations before us, let's add conversations from the younger ones in our breakfast together.

Taylor Maxwell, our oldest son, wrote:

Brilliant Stranger[2]

you're a stranger that's watching over me
when the wind blows fill my sails and set me free
give me vision, something out there i can see
something brilliant. endless skies and hopeful dreams . . .

i've been waiting for my chance to brave the sea
are you watching as the storms fall over me
i'm believing. through the waves the restless seas
you are brilliant. fill my sails and set me free

those eyes those brilliant eyes
i know they're always watching (me)

And seven-year-old Anthem Maxwell, our oldest grandchild, wrote:

---

2   Taylor Maxwell, *Father [& Mother]*, LaunchPad Studios, Inc. 700261335537, 2011, compact disk.

Japan

Close to the river,
raining hard,
the sun is rising
over the town.

Thanks to each of you for coming to breakfast. Imagining all of us together causes me to smile. Knowing my book of poetic confessions includes influence from generations that arrived in the kitchen before me and generations that arrived for breakfast after me, I am humbled and grateful. And I remember again, this time matters.

—Chris Maxwell

introduction: forty years

i barely recall turning forty. when reminded, the events' images appear in my mind, merging a variety of stories and faces, scenes and feelings.

now i'm nearing two decades past forty. memories amalgamate days and weeks, years and decades; pictures redirect me to reality. so do stories. so do poems. these poems. poems of various lengths and styles captured into a collection of one. like a radio station playing various styles for a mixture of genres—rock and country, classical and folk, old and new—these poems portray many moods through my twenties, thirties, forties, fifties.

the number forty, i'm told, biblically symbolizes a period of testing. a trial, a season of waiting, a mystery, a wondering about what is next. mentioned 146 times in Scripture, i'm told, the meaning could, i'm sure, vary. moses isn't here today for an interview, but i'd love to ask his take on forty years in egypt and forty years in the desert—being selected as a rescuer to bring a nation from slavery. to ask spies for details about their glancing for forty days—was the land accessible? to ask jonah about warning nineveh for forty days about potential destruction. or ezekiel being laid on his right side for forty days to symbolize judah's sins. to ask elijah about forty days without food or water at mount horeb. to ask Jesus how He felt and what He thought as He was tempted by the devil during the forty days and nights He fasted as His ministry was about to begin. to ask the followers of Jesus about His noticeable presence for forty days after His resurrection.

the number forty, for me, reveals survival in the quest of life while displaying passion and pain during that endeavor. like most forty day or forty year adventures, and like you, i've known pain. and uncertainty. and love. i've shown that pain and uncertainty and love in verses almost too free at times, and almost too tight at other times, as typing in some strange rhythm served as my rescue and recovery during my realization that all isn't simple in this exploration of life and death and scars and more scars.

scars? forty years of scars?

prayers? forty years of prayers?

confessions? forty years of confessions?

joy? forty years of joy?

yes and yes and yes and yes. and now, this year, this time in my life, we mix these ingredients together in one platter. or, to be specific, we've collected poems and published them. and here they are.

the number forty, for you, might fit the oddity from one of the biblical history lessons. it might fit my own long ride through these streets of sharp turns, steep hills, tiny lanes—these highways under construction requiring me to gallop down roads i never prepared for, never previously traveled on, never yearned to experience. your forty years or forty days might fit a portion of a poem here or a line of a poem there—just because life, like poetry, doesn't follow the design of prose. life is, to me, a poem. a very long and very daunting and very charming poem. life reveals images to us; we feel them. life takes turns, much later letting us finally—and slightly— understand what we previously thought we surely understood. life rhymes at times, then seems to tie nothing together. life is brief and long. life is laughter and tears. life is a surgical procedure. life is waiting and waiting and waiting then noticing the something we waited for occurred unexpectedly right beside us while we stared out the window hoping to glance it from a distance. life thrills us. life scares us.

the number forty, for me, doesn't represent the number on a jersey of a famous athlete or the number of a street or even the years. it carries those parts, but as a whole, at least to me, the number symbolizes grace. to the moses and the jonah in us. to the ezekiel and the elijah in us. from the Jesus in us. wildernesses, deserts, spies, warnings, temptations, days, years. stories poetically revealing ages. poems conversationally intruding normality.

me? i wrote, and write, to survive. i wrote my own method of poetry before and after my brain battled its war as i neared my own forty. and though more words hide now, i'm still writing to survive.

you? thanks for taking a little time in your own wildernesses, deserts, spies, warnings, temptations, days, and years to open your eyes and open your mind and open your heart to taste the stories. i hope you'll love some of the poems. i hope you'll find a place in many of them where your own forty days find a place, where your own forty questions or forty words or forty prayers find a place.

it is, i guess, a matter of time.

my time. your time. this time.

of forty years or forty days or forty words or forty letters.

time, which i've learned through these decades really matters.

so, in the poem of your own life, notice now as one tiny giant that matters greatly in this rapid lane of time.

reflections

i live with severe brain damage. some of these poems were written during my recovery from encephalitis, some were written as i've learned to endure this life of epilepsy and short term memory struggles, and some were written as i reflected on other life issues. writing was one of the best medicines i could have taken.

poetry and words

i'm thankful today for poetry.

the imagery. the rhythm. the sounds. the lines.
reading it, today.
hearing it, now.
daring my damaged brain
to envision, to visualize, to notice,
and then to craft words.
luring my loving heart toward care again.
today. this morning. now.

words open readers' minds to think and feel and wonder.
windows open.
doors open.
moods change, suddenly or slowly.
bright lights begin to dim.
they quickly shine again, then fade.

walking into rooms then out.
running into fields then through.
investigating with and without.
noticing the old and the new.
words which have aged
gracefully, peacefully, appealingly.
words which are waking to life
for the first time, for this time, for now.

this now.
today's morning.
an only time as a reality of itself
but also as a pleasure for repetition.
more moments. more nows. more todays. more mornings
of poetic motion, of pieces and portions, imagery and rhythm.
curving lines through hills and streams.

hearing feet tapping as precision with resolve, with tenacity.
hearing water flowing as a lover racing home.

words. fit. together.

words. fall. apart.

not controlled. not controlling.
it's about noticing.
noticing now, the same.
noticing again, differently.
and again, and differently again.

space covered with these friends of mine.
near me, they stay.
then they hide.
i find them, maybe.
but the process
of sliding downhill on a windy day like today
is fitting.
words are the wind.
words are the weather.
words are the ground.
words are the rain.
words are the heat.
words are the cold.

let us not miss them.
let us not ignore them.
they rhyme at their own times.
they reveal their rhythm in their own ways.
they capture us, as pace and flow and image
dare again our damaged brains and broken hearts to notice.

reality

words spoken or written, intentionally or unintentionally, and released.
words heard or read, passively or aggressively, and received.
words captured, carried, cast away.
words caught, canned, kept in place.

words for now. words for then.
words for us. words for them.

influential, compassionate, aware.
contemplative, aggressive, unsure.

words, describing and defining,
revealing images into many minds,
releasing experiences into many hearts.

welcome words.
learn from, love with, live in words.
speak them when needed.
think and rethink them correctly.
edit them mentally before releasing.

let them heal rather than hurt.
let them gently open doors
rather than slamming shut.
work a craft of respect, humility,
courage, hope, dreams, care,
compassion, and positive influence
through words.

a world is being changed by them.
we are part of that transformation.
i pray our words offer health
rather than harm.
i pray our words alter the

course of damage
and turn toward recovery.

deep care. kind words.
positive change.

even now

you know about those moments, don't you?
those times when you feel sadness but joy is still with you.
those experiences when you detect fear but assurance sits beside you.
those days when external circumstances
just can't defeat inner assurance.
those nights when you're alone but you know you're not really alone.
you know about those moments, don't you?
of peace and love existing in a world of war and division?
of calmness amid the storm?
those moments of inner rest,
even now, no matter what else stares back.
you know, don't you?

uncertain

i'm listening to the dialogue.
i'm hearing all the news.
i'm listening to conversations.
i'm hearing various views.

i'm noticing fearful faces.
i'm seeing through the show.
i'm noticing the expectations.
i'm seeing sorrow grow.

they're unsure about the future.
they're ashamed of life right now.
they're arguing and debating.
they're searching for a "how."

we're ambitious in one moment.
we're holding every breath.
we're alone among our crowds.
we're living like it's death.

my God[3]

moments of a new mentality,
as mysteries make an impression
over all of this, yes, all of this
in me now and on me now.
God knows what has been done and
God knows what to do and
God knows how to do it all;
standing tall,
seeing me and knowing me,
standing tall, a Father forming a future for His child; that is my
God.

---

3   Chris Maxwell, *Changing My Mind* (Franklin Springs, GA:
LifeSprings Resources, 2005) 139.

old ideas for a new life[4]

sad words from a serious God.
serious words from a sad God.
sure words, given years ago, saved until now.
still, within this time, true.
God's disappointment described through
the prophet hosea,
who knew the God who knew sadness.
read this. read this
and wonder. what does this great God think
of us, here,
of us, how
we live after what He has done?
He loves us, yes,
but what do our actions send toward Him?

His Presence, the Spirit of Holiness,
available to live inside us.
His Son, the Christ,
offered in our place.

yet, how will we respond?
the more He called israel
the less they lived love for Him,
the more they left Him.
the more He calls us
what do we do?

there is no call to work to earn salvation,
no commands to impress the Pure King.
the calls equal life: letting Him love us and hold us,
Him living through us, loving through us, lifting us to Himself.
do we hear the call?
what is our response?

---

4   included Hosea 11:1–2 at the beginning and Hosea 12:1–2 at
the end

the substitution story

someone told me an old, old story
about a cross upon a hill.
it left me crying, this tale of dying;
of precious blood that there did spill.
Forsaken Son, the Promised One;
hanging naked, lonely, dead.
He chose to go there, and our sins bear;
a God-man punished in our stead.

the stairway[5]

i stand before the stairway;
its mystery intrigues me,
its height frightens me.
i need to climb;
advancing one step at a time,
slowly but surely
reaching the top,
escaping my bondage,
finding my freedom.
i have attempted the climb before,
never rising past the first few steps.
will now be any different?
will i make it to the top this time
and leave behind
the basement of my futility?
i agree to start,
and i pray that a Gentle Guide
will lift me, walk me,
to the triumph waiting
at the top.

---

5   Psalm 40:1–3

as the Lord promised

none of His promises to moses failed to be born.
all His sayings are trustworthy;
money in the bank,
count on it,
definite,
for sure.

the smallest markings from His pen,
the faintest whispers from His voice,
will live past the end,
will stand through the storm.

abraham, promised a son,
outlived the possibility,
but the many birthdays
could not blow out the candle
of God's promise.
a son laughed his way into the old man's arms
as the Lord promised.

a rainbow ends the thunderstorm
and decorates earth's sky
to capitalize a word to an ancient sailor,
never to bathe the world into oblivion,
and, despite sin and hate,
the earth still stands,
as the Lord promised.

the rabbi hung between two robbers
breathed what appeared to be His last.
but He disarmed death,
and revealed nail-prints,
cooked supper on the shore,

and lived,
and lives,
as the Lord promised.

and you?
have too many birthday cakes been eaten?
does the rain never stop to give a glimpse of the rainbow?
does the Alive One really live?
if so, does He live for you?
will morning bloom from the night of your life
as the Lord promised?

yes,
if He has promised.
He is not obligated to satisfy our selfishness,
only to keep His promises.

yes,
if you do not take the fulfillment into your own hands.
your hands are too small;
you will mess up.

yes,
if you walk in the path of the promise.
biting the forbidden apple expels you from the garden of promise.
the death sentence is our fault;
not His.

what has He then promised for me, for you?
sins can be forgiven.
life can be given
as a gift to the underserving.
our needs can be met inside His heart.
He will not desert us, ever.
reservations in the castle are good forever, and ever.
as the Lord promised.

hidden[6]

can i work the task required of me
for a day of living in the misery
with an outlook toward a joy
so close and far?
the love can shine like the southern sun;
the truth can cut with a surgeon's precision;
the peace can rain like a steady storm.
but why does the trinity of virtues
hide from me so well?

i am needy and alone,
yet, i am complete and never forsaken.
the tension keeps me stranded
between the heaven of tomorrow
and the hell of present pain.
i walk through the door of prayer,
bringing both tears and laughter.
eyes open:
for the Presence of the Holy.

---

6   Psalm 17

seeing

the passive entertainment of the bigness of our efforts
confuses even hopes we once possessed.
a precisely timed maneuver matches all the counter-punches
to proclaim we really are what we professed.
there is no truth in fairy tales, or so the experts say,
those who choose to forget dreams of lesser men,
but here and there a child will see a cloudless sky above him
and sing of days when
love will
love again.

reconstruction

a ram stood beside a canal,
two long horns,
one larger after slow development,
the ram ran unstoppable
west, north, south,
riding as he wished.

his ruling rushed
to an end one day.

a goat,
making statements of strength,
with a single horn,
attacked, defeated, destroyed,
the reigning ram with two horns.

the goat governed
as his horn transformed into four,
one became two,
towering land beautiful,
then blowing away the
beauty of the land,
hoping to hold a planet
in his own hand.

then voices. two voices.
a question plus an answer. desperation,
how long in desolation?
go to bed and rise to eat:
2,300 times.
then the rulers will not rule.
then the temple will return,

---

7   Daniel 8:1–14

then the people can smile again,
when home feels like home.

i was not there then.
i am here now, not near
greece or egypt or asia minor.
i do not hear the sounds
of animals as kings
but i hear a similar voice that
sings, echoing a voice of
ego, power, self.
it can shower down from
any tower, any town
upon the ground
of now and here.

shall we fear?
let's call Hope near.

evenings: we shall rest.
mornings: we shall pray.
through each day
we can allow work to be done
within us.

a vision fulfilled.
a new life found.
me, this me, reconsecrated.
let it be.

a call to prayer

He calls us here.
He meets us here.
do we hear the calling?
do we notice the Presence?

if we come at all,
let us come expecting and desperate,
full of passion and anticipation;
convicted of our sin, convinced of our Savior,
seeking for conversion, searching for Christ.
humble, but hoping.
afraid, but aggressive.
reverent, but relentless.

name the ones we love.
label the pain we hate.
mention the darkness we despise.
discard the chains that choke us.
admit how hard this is,
but learn that it can be done.

He is here and we draw near.

we bow our heads.
we bend our knees.
we wait for a Power that rides the breeze
that blows into a room
where questioning seekers become courageous saints.
still human, but more whole.
still frail, but closer to fine.
still stumbling, but then standing:
standing up, standing still,
standing for Him, standing forever.

Father, watch over me, us, them.
Doctor, ease this relentless pain.
Savior, rescue me.

take this life, these friends, this land;
caress us all inside Your hand.
hold us in Your palm of knowing,
keep us praying, keep us growing.

keep us, we pray.

the shore[8]

the night's presentation declared wonder—a clear spring sky
exposing the beauty of stars smiling. clouds departed. darkness
appearing
friendly, my mind imagined my own constellations.
a wide world imparted images for an imagination to see
in its way, its time, its method.
no longer concealed. revealed.
no longer hidden. exposed.
sensation invited, at least inside me.
while alone.
while thinking.
while dreaming.
while imagining.
perceiving fictional pictures stimulated by nonfictional characters
far away but near on that night,
in my mind,
with me.

should we call it dreaming? thinking? imagining?
should we call it exercising the mental system?

systems keep us stable.
they guide, direct, lure, inspire.
they protect and provide.
they can also become damaged, causing malfunctions in unexpected
times.
they can overreact, causing ongoing storms amid the constellations
of normality.
brains can be systems fitting all those categories.
my brain is.
my brain does.
the mental electrical system—hidden by a bald head and a skull,

8   Chris Maxwell, *Underwater* (Travelers Rest, SC: True Potential Potential, Inc., 2017) 144–145.

masked by prepared agenda and rehearsed smiles,
covered by sincere care and bare confessions—can feel like
a clear sky on a calm night.
but it can change.
it does change.
it becomes—sometimes slowly, sometimes suddenly—a storm.
winds rage.
thunder hits the stage and gets all the attention.
lightning strikes.
from image to reality, what does that mean?
when the brain struggles because of scar tissue,
learning and remembering and communicating
labor to do their assigned duties.
maybe slowly, feeling tired and weak and dizzy.
maybe suddenly, scrambling to stutter a word.
a creative sentence written.
an inspiring phrase stated.
then? a name forgotten, a nap needed, a mood shifting,
an emotion appearing like a cloud barging in to redesign a sky's beauty
on a lovely evening in georgia.

though it has issues,
i try hard to work well with this mind of mine.
i know her weaknesses, her tendencies, her barriers.
she strives to overcompensate for her scars.
the obsession with work overworks her as she seeks to locate words hidden
deep inside her damaged region.

but my mind moved away from herself and dwelled again on the marvel above.
for then, she just gazed at the sky's grace.
she needed a moment, gazing at a sky smiling down,
telling her and telling me
to rest, to be still, to just be.

that is how i feel coming ashore.
leaving, for a moment, the waves of epilepsy.

confessions

whether seeing a counselor, confessing to a priest,
crying while telling painful stories to a trusted
friend at dinner, or visiting clergy to find reasons
for our questions, we all need someone to talk to.
we need to release inner hurt. poetic journaling
has been one of my methods of facing grief and
finding recovery.

slow God

God is, at least from my perspective, slow.
He offers an idea; it shocks those who hear Him
tell mesmerizing angles of what will occur.
then? nothing.
days pass. weeks pass. years pass. decades pass.
i expected forty minutes until the shift from
revelation to reality,
but forty days or weeks or years?
for us, or at least for me, way too long.
that is forever.

God is, also, sudden.
though working leisurely, from our view,
though acting sluggishly, if at all,
though fulfilling His own promises slowly, in hiding,
the long awaited action occurs rapidly.
many actions seem to happen all at once,
after the waiting-on-this-forever-season surprisingly ended.
a slow and sudden God, i consider we can call Him.
for us, or at least for me, that is good.
that is very good.

who cares?

"who cares?," he asked,
voicing a question,
desiring to find
someone who cares about
a person or a cause.
those two words through him, though,
didn't carry that meaning.
in the context of his question,
eyes rolling repeatedly and
forehead adding redness in
a hurry, his meaning
wasn't that meaning.

he asked who cares intending to reveal his
lack of care of
anyone else's view.

but care can, at times,
mean care.

people can, by choice,
choose care.

true care for others, that
too-often-missing component
from leaders who drive to accomplish,
is healthy and hopeful.
care is like a cure.
people crave the medication
of care,
desiring what feels distant,
hoping for deep listeners,
genuine lovers,

gentle shepherds,
kind mentors,
true friends at one table
where diverse backgrounds merge into single stories.

but care isn't to be carried.
care doesn't mean obsessed or controlled.
love hurts, as it should.
it wounds, as it should.
but love can cause deeper damage
when not balanced with self-care and sabbath,
when not protected by receiving love.

care. each day, intensely.
but do not carry
the weight of others' burdens.
care for them and help them learn to release, to receive.
listen, and let go.
love and bleed a little,
but
glance at the sky and realize all is not up to you.
breathe deeply and rest well,
knowing that you are
the one who cares but not the one who carries.

who cares? we do.
who carries? no one
should carry alone.
our mental and emotional
muscle can't hold the weight of our worries.
bearing burdens of friends
is good.
continually keeping those burdens is not good.
finding balance
brings deep care
without control.

care deeply.
release intentionally.
emotions eventually
will follow; you will find
peace in the caring.

proof

irrevocable evidence, a required demand,
doesn't always arrive.
a few minds, or many minds, depend on it.
belief without such proof, they say,
isn't wise.

i find evidence, beyond enough for
me, nearby.

staring up,
my eyes see a bright sun doing her
job, displaying
her effort of proof.

breathing deeply, the repetition of
inhale and exhale, slowly,
inhale and exhale, slowly,
inhale and exhale, slowly,

calming myself
doesn't qualify as apologetics,
but lures a smile, my smile,
supplying assurance.

listening to stories, their stories,
in this office of books and more books,
memories and more memories,
offers my own confirming nod
about an Artist creating and continuing
to craft His art.

faces. wind.
an ocean's waves rushing ashore then away.
voices. rain.
a mountain's size of height and depth.

aroma. trees.
a world of wonder, of beauty, of life
near me, with me, around me, showing me
proof of all i need to see to believe.

others doubt about the Artist, that One
Who crafted and continues crafting
the brains of those questioning His
existence. i don't see His face, but i believe
He smiles.
He cares,
i believe, for each doubter
and each believer, as He continues
crafting each one,
each day, each moment,
nearby, near us and now,
near those believing,
near those doubting,
near those seeking convincing proof.

evidence so close but ignored
and rushed past.
a smile. His love.
for all.

where is God?[9]

my jerking face, my shaking lips, my wet eyes, my uncontrolled
remarks:
where was God during that time?
maybe He told me where, and i just couldn't recall.
maybe i already knew but just couldn't remember.
since my ears received sound waves
but got little help from the brain's reception,
maybe God's answer remained undiscovered in mysterious terrain.
i could only pray and hope God heard.
pray and hope.
pray. and hope.
i thought of my thinking
as i worked to realize and remember.

---

9   Chris Maxwell, *Changing My Mind* (Franklin Springs, GA:
LifeSprings Resources, 2005) 18.

wishing [10]

imagine a room with three windows. walk toward one.
as you open the blinds and glance through the window,
you notice your past.
you had expected to see a normal day:
the birds outside, maybe a rabbit, a light drizzle,
a picnic table in the back.
but you saw faces, felt feelings, heard songs,
and smelled the fragrance from years ago.
imagine backing up and moving toward your next window.
this one doesn't allow you to see outside.
the screen reflects your face. you see yourself.
you notice the now, the present.
you're glancing at the countenance of who you are.
you take a few steps back and walk to window three. you slowly,
slowly, slowly—unsure of what you might notice—open the
window blinds.
there you see what you assume is your future.
you observe yourself older,
walking with a few people you suppose are friends.
think now about the three windows.
through which window would you prefer to continue glancing?
which scenes bring fear, pain, joy, anger, hope, healing?
which views convey caution or courage or compassion? why?
a visit to the past can motivate us toward anger and resentment.
or joy and celebration.
or a mixture of each extreme.
or maybe very little—if we've chosen to hide our days
of pain by living in denial.
the same for the now—we can celebrate the present
or seek to deny the moments of now.
and for the future we can fear entering new land

---

10   Chris Maxwell, *Pause: The Secret to a Better Life, One Word at a Time* (Travelers Rest, SC: True Potential, 2012) 235–236.

or we can anticipate an adventure of wonder.
take time to glance out the windows.
remember the past.
forgive and be forgiven.
notice the pain and be healed. smile.
discern the present. stare through
incorrect assumptions and improper perceptions.
see you. believe in the Creator Who made you,
the Father Who loves you. accept the face
looking back and make a choice. smile at yourself.
dream of the future. good dreams.
big dreams. impossible dreams.
dream with faith, anticipation, potential, and an eternal family.
and, make the choice again: smile.
as you depart and leave the windows, remember what you noticed.

praying[11]

praying. segments of time dedicated to dialogue with God.

praying. moments of asking and receiving, singing and listening,
reading and studying, watching and noticing,
thinking and waiting, hoping and doubting.

praying. pausing in a hurried, demanding, angry, dangerous,
risky, selfish, clingy, wide, tiny, confusing, conflicting, sour,
wounded, deceitful, political, swift, stunning, holy world.

praying. slowing down just a little and noticing
the two deer run by the yard early on a
monday morning as the rain patters the ground again,
as that week's schedule feels intimidating,
as a strange inner peace adds a smile to the observer's moist face.

praying. refusing to respond too quickly as the emotions
become strong,
but choosing instead to step aside for a moment
to reflect, to release, to request
help from the Comforter.

praying. responding to the bad news with pleas
of desperation amid
questions of uncertainty
and all the faith you can muster.

praying. glancing at the list.
mentioning each need—some more than once.
believing the requests are being heard and will be answered.

---

11   Chris Maxwell, Pause for Moms: Finding Rest in a too Busy
World (Travelers Rest, SC: True Potential, 2013) 207–209.

praying. a part of history.
an act in the present.
an invitation to affect the future.
an honored but often forgotten privilege.
a welcome. a sacred treasure.

praying. a confession of sin. an appeal for help.
a statement of desperation. a declaration of triumph.

praying. in a closet. in a bedroom. in the shower.
in the car. on a plane. on the treadmill.

praying. my father saying the blessing before each meal.
one grandfather taking me on walks by the railroad track
and my grandmother sitting beside me with a smile.
one grandfather reminding me of the beauty of prayer while
working outside
and my grandmother praying while cooking and cooking
and cooking.

praying. a pastor staring
at the empty auditorium and praying for God to speak
through him in two hours.

praying. a doctor entering surgery not knowing if his patient
will survive.

praying. in the doctor's office when
you hear him say that word you hoped to never hear: cancer.

praying. a mother holding her child—
not feeling any heart beats, not feeling any breaths, not feeling
any circulation,
not understanding why God did not heal this child so many people
prayed for.

praying. a family reunion—with food and tension.
finally, the two who haven't spoken in a long time speak.
just a few words. but words. kind words.

praying. sitting in the bathroom listening to the hurricane sound
like an engine
moving closer and closer and closer to the father, mother, and
two sons.
the immobile house seemed to be moving.
one son, after praying the Lord's prayer and quoting the twenty-
third psalm,
asked, "are we sure i'm going to heaven if i die?"

praying. as she takes the car to the mechanic. again.
waiting for the bad news while knowing she can't pay bills
this month,
her ex won't pay child support, her grass needs to be cut,
and her son needs a dad. how will she drive to work?

praying. every time he drives past the church. he never stops but
he prays every time. will he ever stop?

praying. for the habit, the lure, the addiction to end. she thought it
had ended but her desire has returned. in the car
afraid of where she's going, while praying.

so many pray in so many ways.

life and love and pain. happy prayers and sad prayers.

intercession—when they ask God to help other people.
petition—when they ask God for specific things.
thanksgiving—when they thank God for His goodness to them.

silence and supplication and meditation and study and
contemplation and research and listening—and so many
other methods
of praying, of engaging in dialogue with God.

so many ways to pray.
so many things to pray about.

but praying isn't always easy. we tend to stray away from it.
in our hurry, in our self-obsessed inner-world, in our gaze toward
defeat, in our
i-must-do-something-instead-of-being-lazy-and-asking-God-to-do-
it-for-me world,
praying isn't easy.

it is needed, though.
prayer is engaging in the most healthy and most needed
chat possible.

unfailing love[12]

unfailing love.
is that possible?
at times, love seems to be
synonymous with failure.
here today, gone tomorrow.
love, strong and true and determined,
turns into a selfish, tainted, demanding monster.

wedding rings are sold
to pay the divorce attorneys.

but, the poet speaks of
unfailing love.
yes, it is possible
because it flows from the fountain
of God's holy, unchanging character.

let it flow my way, o God.

with salvation riding its currents,
let it flow.

help me trust You and Your love,
and then be able to answer
the ones who taunt me,
the ones unaware such a river runs,
the ones for whom love seems to fail.

---

12   Psalm 119:41–42

joy in the morning

a tapestry of tragedy
decorates my once so peaceful life,
captures my attention,
demands my energy.
i watch.
and i pray.

dark night of my soul;
venturing outside the boundaries
of clock, of calendar, of comfort:
toil ticking on and on.
dark dawn,
dark day,
dark dusk;
another night,
dark night of my soul.

are you friend or foe?
are you angel or demon?
are you from the hand of God?
        to speak or to shape?
        to break or to make?
are you from the hand of liar?
        to steal, kill, destroy?

yet, i will sing through the pain,
through the chains;
salvation will come:
His promise is proof,
past provision is proof;
He has not forgotten.

finite anger; infinite favor.
i now taste the flavor
of a new perspective;

knowing the limits placed on weeping,
growing a harvest for the keeping,
flowing from planting to reaping;
the results of endurance,
the development of character,
the maturing of this child.

dark night,
a labor of anguish,
gives birth to a new day;
a day without tears,
replacing the fears.
perfect vision beyond the past tensions.
looking now i see both rhyme and reason;
all questions not answered,
but a calm assurance overshadows the traumatic moments,
a bright sun replaces the black sky.

the dark night of my soul
ends with the piercing alarm of my Father's will.
now i am better, not bitter;
rescued from the edge of hell,
robbed from the grave,
raised from the pit.
His large and loving hand
scared me, but saved me;
scarred me, but soothed me.

now, at this conclusion:
a new beginning,
a new me.
trading in the ball and chain,
slipping into dancing shoes:
let the music play;
i take the hand of my Partner
and enjoy His Presence.

a tapestry of triumph
decorated my once so painful life,
captures my attention,
demands my energy.
i grow.
and i praise.

criticism[13]

cheap shots from the gallery
wear you down
over time.

at first, you are prepared,
and the initial attacks
meet the resistance
of zeal and determination.

the questions come
and you listen
and you learn
or you laugh.

but, like a boxer
tiring from
repeated body blows,
you weaken.

you've taken much
and would now love
to retaliate.

you need the Spirit
that sustained Christ
and kept Him quiet
and kept Him going
to the cross.

let God be God.

trying to take His place
will kill you faster
than the
cheap shots from the gallery.

13   Matthew 5:11–12

addiction[14]

groping still
for coping skills
that permanently alter pain.
too often the ticks
only complicate the tension
plunging me into a maze
of hostile design
and hidden doubt;
nailing me to the scaffold
of relentless pursuit
and restless poverty.
as endless debts accrue
i don't know what to do;
my cleverness perishes in a
demanding deluge of
alienation, consequences,
obligation and simulation.
masks cover hurt only on the surface.
medication numbs affliction only for a season:
a short season. a season
that melts into a reality of
greater grief and growing guilt.
within and without.
so close and so far.
victory and defeat
i groan for redemption, for release.
can i live here?
will help arrive before it's too late?

---

14   Romans 7:7–25

success

success is not what it seems:
giants shrink and beauty fades,
money slips through the fingers.
to envy the wicked
one must stare too long at the visible
and ignore the invisible,
the inevitable,
the consequences lurking around the corner.
they may thrive now,
but they have one hell of a future.

trust, depend, believe,
rely on the Lord.
give attention to Him, not to the wicked.
keep Him in focus,
that is the substance of your hope,
the proof of the imperceptible.
delight yourself in Him, enjoy,
taste and be satisfied.

walk hand-in-hand with the Shepherd,
then you will do good.
doing good is the result of faith, trust, reliance;
not the cause.
behavior flows from the fountain of belief.
the sun will rise to interrupt the night,
its heat will shine at high noon:
thus will be our right doing,
your character, your person.

right now? claim a promise for the moment?
wait a minute,
an hour, a day.   a decade;
but wait,
still and patient,

not fretting or losing focus.
evil emerges from wrath,
from wickedness, from worry.
an inheritance grows
from the waiting;
the gift of peace and purity,
an internal plot of promised land.

but when? a while,
a little while.
God's time or mine?
when the time is right
the one who rules his own life
will vanish,
leaving no forwarding address;
the one who lets God rule his life,
as victor,
will move into his new home.

evil men plotting, scheming,
grinding, hating;
God laughing:
He has the last word.
the sword they use to cut down others
will soon slice them into pieces.

poverty is worth more than prosperity
and powerlessness than power,
if God holds the poor one, the powerless one.
God knows the poor,
though no one else seems to,
He knows them—
their days, their nights,
their endless fights
to eat, breathe, sleep.
He knows.

God will extinguish the evil one,
the thief, the smooth-talker,
the sound-bite savior
who preys upon the weak.
God curses them;
He calls them every name in the book.
He cuts them off.
the righteous ones,
who feel so cut off, so estranged,
He will uphold, establish, sustain.

i stumble, He lifts me.
i fall, He picks me up.
they don't love me; He loves me.
He holds my hand.

look to the east, the west,
the present, the past.
to the givers He will give,
from the takers He will take.
the humble, the generous, the dependent;
He will assist. they will not starve.
even if their portions stay small until death,
beyond that curtain waits a banquet table;
they will not be forsaken.

repent, o son of adam;
change your mind, your direction,
and do good.
He will keep you, love you,
protect you, provide for you.
speak wisdom, justice;
search the law and live therein.

though the wicked desire you
and plan to devour you,
God has the last word.
they will be destroyed soon,

in a bad way.
God will bless soon,
in a big way.

salvation and safety,
providence and promise,
hope and help;
gifts placed in the hands open,
open in surrender to the will of the Giver.

we are bonded

*w*alking into the sunlight together,
*e*scaping the cruel darkness that has haunted us.

*a*ware of the dangers, though somewhere numbed by passion,
*r*ich and full,
*e*ver sure of such a strange uncertainty.

*b*ravery assumes the driver's seat
*o*f this vehicle of caring.
*n*o one else knows me, sees me, loves me;
*d*are to proceed? or will we cower,
*e*asing out of love and into less-than-life?
*d*o not run. stay with me. and i will stay with you.

a plea; a bargain

strong chord:
live creature;
increases augmentation.
eyes—never focused.
ears—ignoring the silence.
mind—racing, racing.
heart—in pieces.
i was directed
toward a road of yellow bricks,
paved with vision,
traversed with hope, with longing.
on this trip
the journey develops the dream.
as one walks toward desire,
desire appears unexpectedly.

i'll rip down the sign on my life.
the property is not private.
trespass the territory,
invade me now,
make me new,
make me different,
make me Yours,
make a difference.

the gate[15]

the gate is closed.
does it keep me out
or in?
is it for protection
or prohibition?
do i have an enemy
that would attack
if the gate
did not block entry?
am i the enemy
lurking in pursuit
of a land i dare not enter?
i did not latch the gate,
and i cannot unlock it.
i cannot break through:
its strength is too great.
i cannot climb over;
it is far too tall.
possibly, i should accept the existence
of the gate
and find contentment
on this side.

---

15   Psalm 19:7–11

powerless[16]

are you still wondering how they could do that?
do you still sit in judgment,
assuming they were beyond such a mistake?
we should know human nature better than that;
we should know our tendency toward wickedness,
our affinity with wrong,
our habits of hate.
have you looked in the mirror lately?
have you been honest about the evil lurking
in the shadows of your own heart?
in the shattered glass,
in pieces at our feet:
a reminder of who we were and what we are
and what we would be without Him.

the dilemma: sinful nature vs. spiritual man.
condition? i am unspiritual.
confusion? i do not understand.
conflict? a war raging within.
culprit? sin,
that demanding tyrant, so consistent and powerful,
hungry for death, thirsty for pain,
thriving on the weakness of my flesh.

the description: sins of commission and omission.
thank you, paul; i'm glad i am not alone.
we do what we do not want to do.
we do not do what we want to do.
this powerless desire to do right
needs the strength of One Who can do right.

---

16   Romans 7:14–25

the despair: searching for an answer.
two key considerations that open us to answers,
to truth, to hope, to Kingdom success.
a realization: what a wretched man i am!
the first step to victory is an admission of defeat.
in this miserable, distressed condition
i recognize my inability.
i am powerless to help myself,
so i fall face down before a Holy God
who deserves the best but accepts me at my worst
if i admit my wickedness and agree to His terms for change.
a question: who will rescue me from this body of death?
not "what can i do differently," or "how can i be better,"
but, "who will be my Deliverer?"
a drowning man needs a Rescuer;
he needs to stop the fighting, the splashing and kicking,
giving in to the strength and wisdom of the One
Who guards his life and swims him to safety.

the deliverance: salvation in Jesus.
thanks be to God, freedom,
through Jesus Christ our Lord.

here, but not really[17]

a cage, heart-prison, my security;
a rage growing in obscurity;
a page turning to day and place.
priorities of present time and space
reverse inside the Truth,
remain off center inside the mind.

climbing trees for a distant glimpse;
touching threads for an imparted gift:
how far will i go?
i'm not the type
to step outside the boat,
to drop in through the roof,
to shout when told to be silent,
to watch when sleep comes knocking.
or am i?
should i be?

predictability, my long lost friend,
taught me well and ruined me.
gratification, my silent shadow,
steers me,
possesses many lives,
never dies.

is there room upon the tree
for a thief that looks like me?

live for immortality
or hang in anonymity.
turn the corner on this moment;
dare to stare inside this gift;

---

17   Romans 8:18–27

ripped open, yet concealed;
in my grasp, yet far away.
will i see the light better when night falls?
will i run faster on my knees?

tears drop; the waters rise.
heart beats; the earth quakes.
before sleep settles the alarm screams,
but even in morning the self dreams
of one day soon
beyond the moon,
the day after time,
the street past the end:
arms open and table spread;
smiling, singing, knowing . . .

then the light shows red,
the cars slow,
i put on brakes and wonder
who chose red for stop.
i quit dreaming and turn on the radio.
i live here but not really.
i love here but not really.
i drive on
looking through a dirty windshield.

my car still isn't running right.

joining in the struggle[18]

having a struggle; wish you were here.
but, that's how it is when you live with *hope*.
paul lived with hope,
a hope that he would see his fellow believers soon,
a hope that the saints would contribute,
a hope that they would experience all the blessings of Christ.
some live without hope,
sure that the absence of hope will
insulate them from the disappointment of defeat.
in an emotional coma,
they guard their wishes,
disregard their joys,
and live expecting the worst.
then, so they reason, they cannot be let down.
they feel much better since they gave up hope.
not paul.
he had hope for glory in himself:
the indwelling Christ.
he had a blessed hope for the future:
the coming Christ.
like abraham, he had an ongoing hope
undaunted by circumstances and external odds:
the word of God.
like the writer of hebrews,
paul's soul was anchored by hope.
like the psalmist,
paul knew that the cure for a downcast soul
was the placing of hope in God.
living with hope is a struggle.
people fail to keep promises,
situations block you from living your dreams,
friends desert you,

---

18   Romans 15:23–33

prayers are sometimes answered with a "no"
or a long incubation period before a "yes" hatches,
wishes are shattered by a painful dose of reality;
yes, hoping is a struggle.
but, it is the attitude of the follower of Christ.
not optimism, but realism that
adds the numbers of God's character
and God's word to every equation of life.
david hoped in God; goliath lost his head.
elijah hoped in God; the false prophets fell.
daniel hoped in God; the lions purred like kittens.
Jesus hoped in God; death lost the ultimate battle.
the struggle of hope is much better than the sin
of expecting nothing from God.

having a struggle; wish you were here.
but, that's how it is when you live with *prayer*.
paul invited his friends to join in his struggle
by praying for him.
he urged them, recruiting them not with phrases
filled with public relations gems,
but by appealing to Christ and the Holy Spirit.
is Christ Lord?
do they love the Spirit,
and allow the Spirit's love to guide them?
if so, then pray.
it is a struggle,
a wrestling match,
a light vs. dark war for the souls of men,
this struggle of prayer.

it is singing with david about the Lord Who is shepherd,
it is crying with david about the pain in our bodies,
it is screaming with david about the prosperity of the wicked,
it is repenting with david about the sin that invaded our hearts.
it is praying like daniel with his windows open,
it is paul and silas with the jail doors closed.
it is Jesus in the garden.

it is wesley, hyde, finney and luther.
it is murray and ravenhill.
it is a lifestyle, a walk, a struggle.

if we are followers of Christ, we must pray.
we will not grow,
we will not bear fruit,
we will not make it,
unless we join the struggle of prayer.

having a struggle; wish you were here.
but, that's how it is when living with *ministry*.
paul's total dedication to God's work
hindered the realization of personal desires.
it introduced him to stonings, beatings, imprisonment,
ridicule, poverty, shipwreck,
and many other things not on the job description.
do you want to minister?
it is the greatest life, but ready yourself for a struggle.
work for God and people will laugh,
as the wood is shaped into an ark,
as the temple grows in size,
as you cry out for repentance,
as you call fisherman to be your disciples,
as a prostitute gives you a foot massage.
they will support you—then gossip behind your back.
they will work with you—then leave you.
but, you keep hoping and praying and ministering
for God, for His Kingdom,
because of His calling.
paul sought to both give and receive refreshment
from his ministry partners.
if you give but are not given to in return, do not fear,
for great is the reward in heaven
for those who struggle on earth.
hoping, praying, ministering:
having a great time; wish you were here.

remembering another life

today i remember how we talked daily in our former lives. i didn't expect death in that life. but death comes by the choice of one— distancing and silencing and changing and nothing.

huge decisions shocked me and scared me. i didn't expect now to be like it is—this life so sad, so distant, so different. i knew better than to care so much. but i did. so now, today in this new life, i remember that life of then. i remember regular conversations. i remember a voice of care. i recall. and i cry.

mama's goal

though short in stature you stood so tall;
so big—that precious smile.
inside you were a tower of strength.
you'd go the second mile.

you shouldered a load that seemed too much
for even the strong to bear.
your strength came from the One Who said
He always would be there.

you told us all about His Word;
your stories warmed our nights.
when you were near our fears would fade;
the darkness turned to light.

our days would start when we would hear
you sing a cheerful song
to wake us up and send us out,
and teach us right and wrong.

i will never forget those final days
when your body grew so weak;
your spirit soared to greater heights,
saying what you could not speak.

if i could take the love you lived
and shine it all around,
the world would see the Savior's love
and hear the joyful sound.

the goal of your life was to be like Him
Who gave His life for you;
now by His grace i'll walk that road
and make it my goal too.

confusion of this life

illustrations are intended to,
well, illustrate.

but i am focused on my plans for tomorrow.
i'll be boarding a plane and flying south,
entering a journey from present location to future destination.

carry on. luggage. size and weight and ingredients.
life terms. more than phrases for flights.
do we mean what we are saying?
do we mean what we are praying?
do we mean what we are singing?

i arrived. i experienced. i talked. i told stories.
you listened, i believe, to my illustrations illustrating my confusion
of this life flight.

i had never met you or you or you
but i, somehow,
let you and you and you
know me,
well and deeply,
know me
and hear my story
as i heard your stories.

masks removed, we told stories.
we followed guidelines and instructions
while experiencing constructions
of inner healing.

healing, that word
we know and don't know.
we, us now, composed, as one, together.
but only briefly.

respecting perspectives.
interstate closed for repairs.

mental art takes a start
through creativity's
adventure of design
amid dreaming.

thoughts walk regularly and
merge many moods
in seconds.

encephalitis. spell the word.

those days and these days.

so much i would be telling you if we were still communicating.
so much i would be asking you if we were still communicating.

her eyes rolled in my direction;
she didn't like what i had stated, and
she said so
with that reflection.

the coming and the going.
the guessing and the knowing.
our doubt and our faith
travel together in this adventure of mystery.

i remembered, accurately i think, three weeks of rain in georgia.
the sun surprised me yesterday when it came back up. clouds had
covered us
but the beauty of the shine's brightness reminded me maybe all my
hurts aren't
the end of the story.
maybe, hidden by clouds of pain, the warmth remains.

different times and deferent faces.
fresh stories about brand new faces.

on my way, maybe.
here soon, maybe.

conversations

we talk often. we listen sometimes. writing poetic
journals about dialogue helped and helps me to
listen well. but while writing, some portions of my
self-talk came out, revealing thoughts and feelings
i didn't know were there. join the dialogue with
the world, with God, and with yourself.

now standing

standing now,
even uncertain of the
future direction or the
original foundation.
life's rather tricky,
while certainty only
appearing occasionally
during the adventure.

some assurance stands up
and helps us rest
and breathe deeply, calmly,
while thoughts ramble
from one side to another

all while
lowering expectations
to avoid hurt,
or embracing potential
to pursue the risks.

when we give our best
and take that holy chance,
it's like
standing now
in the land of maybes,
of hope held
by hands capable to
somehow carry.

initial hopes stand by fear.
dreams sleep in the night
of favor.
the flavor of invisible reality

tastes like what we've craved for a
very long ride.

life waits.
worlds wait.

we choose.
and are glad.

luggage

after cancelled flights and delayed flights
and calmly panicking
as a flight finally welcomed me
there, i flew and landed
and arrived
but my
luggage did not
arrive with me.
it remained
behind. far away, miles away, states away,
it remained
there instead of here
where needed.

but here,
in our gathering of meals and meetings,
of smiles and conversations,
of dreaming and connecting,
of caring and daring,
we enjoyed time together.
luggage we bring to our audiences
now, in these days of us or them,
right or left,
now or then,
here or there,
ancient or modern, together.

ecstatic challenges and inspiring harmony.
movie screening and educational workshops.
politics and Scripture and hot topics and controversial topics
and needed topics and relevant topics
and luggage arriving.
honest conversations.
appealing meals.
intriguing revelations of varying opinions.

agreeing to disagree
and love
and learn.
welcome a willingness to
sit beside one another at the
table of information and inspiration
in this room of division.
tribes merge,
mingling stories and stats
of news of now.
where many others build walls of worth,
there we design stories of art,
creatively crafting truth.

together now, listening.
together now, learning.
together now, eating
our meals and asking our questions
and telling our stories
and promoting our products
and improving our crafts
to more effectively
affect this culture of
division and fear.

in fresh aromas,
like meals slowly cooking,
we serve as chefs, gladly.

and luggage arrives
on time, or eventually,
in place.

magnetic resonance imaging[19]

staring at a screen
is normal
in our image-driven culture.
but on that early morning in a dim room,
i gazed at an image which proved to
not be normal.
white gray segments revealed
a problem—just their appearance
differed from the darker portions
considered correct. the
how-it-shouldn't-look depiction
was a visual reminder
of me and my struggle
to remember.
before my eyes looked at the computer screen,
revealing realities of the world within my skull,
i lay down for thirty-five minutes—not allowed
to move, only breathing
and praying and thinking
while feeling and hearing forceful percussion.
trapped in that place of investigation and revelation,
i rested. i actually felt peaceful
in that peculiar cabinet;
instead of seeing it as a test to reveal my condition,
i had learned to embrace it for a sabbath.
i recalled previous *mris*, wondering
if the damage to my brain
would be the same
or worse
or better.
i remembered when encephalitis initiated

19   Chris Maxwell, *Underwater* (Travelers Rest, SC: True Potential
Potential, Inc., 2017) 32–33.

all these tests and almost caused
my life on earth to end.
my thoughts traveled in circles from
past to present to future—all while waiting
to view the latest news on my brain.

this brain of mine—scars creating crafty artwork through
the left temporal lobe—needs to settle
on a thought.
if it wavers too soon it might never return. repetition and
concentration and simple instructions
help its ability
to grasp,
to maintain,
to understand,
to retain,
to explain.
on that day, and in that passageway of exploration,
my thoughts dwelled only on themselves
for a while
as the *mri*'s back-and-forth rhythms continued exposing
their effort to know me
so i settled on thoughts
about thinking. about my brain,
though severely damaged,
still an astonishing work of design.
about the brain's parts, all team players hoping to win.
about the brain's weaknesses when damaged,
something i know well.
about the methods of recollection,
seeking to hold on to a noun
or a number
or an encounter
or a person
before escaping into my land of forgetfulness.

while a magnetic field and radio waves labored for useful diagnostic
information,
i just thought.
while not able to move at all,
i just thought about thinking—
of these mysteries we are,
of these brains at work,
of these methods of remembering.

new glasses

eating dinner with a friend
who was wearing his new glasses
revealed that his vision
needed help seeing
through this lens
to get a better view,
to see correctly.

i listened again to his words
and his stories—
a contradiction of reality and self-talk,
of lies and truth,
of deeply planted condemnation
and reality of love and acceptance.

two extremes
battling internally and externally.

we ate dinner.
we talked.
i watched people greet my friend.
they smiled,
revealing the joy they felt
just to see his face,
displaying grace in dialogue,
hitting rewind
and visiting past experiences,
memories of joy.

eating dinner and tasting my food
i could hear conversations of pleasure,
so opposite of the conversations he plays
in the stations of his brain.

i dared my friend to change channels.
i pleaded with my friend to shift quickly,
then, right then,
to begin listening to
words of grace,
words of confirmation,
words of encouragement.

maybe he needs new glasses
in a different way.

precepts[20]

the hungry long for food.
the thirsty for a drink.
the lost long to be found.
the poor to grow rich.

the ones with no purpose, no mission, no objective,
long for an enduring principle,
an unchanging fact,
a truth.

if they find the precepts of God
they find such an absolute,
such a promise.

if they fall to the ground in
the land of truth
they can grow;
a new person,
a new reason,
a new life.

God will harvest a crop of righteousness
from the seeds of sinful ones
who die to themselves
and sprout in the soil
of solid truth.

---

20   Psalm 119:40

the naked Truth

rain dampens the streets while the cars pass.
transients line the walkways in their daily
parade to the library, the park, the plasma center,
the mission: these faces, tired and weathered
faces, without names or histories or futures known
to those of us who belong to the society they're
no longer a part of.

black kids scramble from the bus,
walking several miles to places called home.
they carry no books, just ghetto blasters, smiles,
a worn basketball and a bag of potato chips; the music is loud.
a business man, white man, walks on the grass
as he passes them; they have left no room on the sidewalk.
he does not speak.
they do not speak.

he climbs up the steps into his office with his briefcase in his arm.
they walk, with their music, home.

i look around the room, this room, and no one knows
me. i know no one. we are, each of us, shackled
by the chains of our own importance, and we like it that way.
i am me and you are you.
i do my thing and you do yours.
here is the line; i dare you to cross it.

isn't that, this crossing of the line, what Jesus did?
He dared to cross it and then to challenge its very existence.
maybe that's why we do not like Jesus very much.
oh, we "love" Him and "serve" Him and "worship" Him.
we are experts at such efforts; we are religion professionals.
but, on a relational level, on the level of
sharing a laugh with Him, doing lunch with Him, being with Him
without talking or singing or doing anything,

that's when we have trouble.
we do not enjoy
activities that contain little activity—just
me being me
with Him.
that says we dislike Him.
we have trouble liking anyone who invades our space
and questions our motives. He has a way of seeing through
our clothes of hurry and excellence and industry
and brilliance to see that we are naked.
completely naked. we aren't pleased with that
because we are ashamed of ourselves.
like the emperor, we're all naked.
like the little boy,
Jesus is the only One with the courage, the honesty,
to tell us so.

well, let's not dwell too long on such thoughts.
there are people here. it's raining outside
and i have an appointment in half an hour.

living and dying

working, watching, waiting, wanting on and on;
to numb myself through lies could never heal the hurt
that never exits home beneath the surface of myself:
the self i know and don't know; so clean, so full of dirt.
smile through sadness, love through hate, laugh through salty tears,
i've heard the shouts of death and felt the chill of cold.
i've died a death in springtime. i've seen a day at night.
i've been a sort of help to men or so i have been told.

clutching hopes of peace i run to cash them into proof
but the stops seem far too many, the mountains far too high.
shall i hold my head up and pretend that all is fair,
or hold it high believing my redemption drawing nigh?

she came and left and then one came and one more after that.
was it truth or just a lie that left me so alone?
He came too and He left too and is said to come again
and offer flight to all who dream of a world unknown.

home's a place or home's a face or home's no home at all
when the place is cold or the face too old or carefully unreal.
place it on the table, all you who dare to die to live:
escaping feelings to once again be aware of how to feel.
the love of joy, the joy of love, the kindness and the songs,
the heart and mind and spirit, the inside of a friend;
beginnings start you over and faith continues on
but will there be a one of us still loving at the end?

real love

God's love is action, the proper thing done.
God's love is a person, the one Perfect One.
love is patient, love is kind;
love is more than a state of mind.

love, the verb, is what i do.
not seeking self, but serving you.
it reaches in to then reach out.
it doesn't boast, it doesn't pout.
protecting, hoping, lasting long,
pursuing right, rejecting wrong.
when feelings fade and faults appear,
love, the verb, will persevere.

love, the noun, is a gift called grace;
it's God come down in a human face.
with hands to heal, to help, to hold;
compelling compassion—a God to behold.
love unto dying, a King ever living,
never denying the gift ever giving.
love is the life, the good news we tell;
love, the noun, is Emmanuel.

God's love upon becomes God's love within
for us to give, so let us begin.
love is patient, love is kind;
love is always right on time.

observations

most of us hurry past too many lovely moments.
these poems were attempts at noticing the wonder
nearby. forcing myself to slow my pace, i noticed.
i stared. i listened. i napped. i fell in love with the
often ignored.

shaking of the head

have you noticed?
i have.
i did.
and i will, i hope,
remember being noticed
unexpectedly, during
an interruption that caused
my head to shake
as my heart smiled.
the shaking of the head
is a statement being said,
though what is
revealed can vary,
depending on the context and intent.

a head can shake
to say no, or
to display frustration, or
to relay the message of fear, or
to show a feeling of being surprised.
the first and simple shaking of a head
might include
determined eyes or
might include
an afraid face
as the shaking is saying no.
frustration can also be a cause of that movement,
when anger or exhaustion or
disagreement or resentment
or an inner war, still unknown,
leads to movement of the body and head.
fear can cause shaking
of hands and heart and face,

as can doubt,
and depression,
and denial.

but occasionally
a head shakes when surprised by joy,
when hearing of news too good, almost, to be true.
my head shook that way.
i didn't expect a person
to say
what he said to me,
about me.
not demanding the who i should become
but declaring the who i
already am.
the voice was firm but kind.
the face stared at me
and stated what i hope is true
but often feels so distant.
my head shook
out of surprise.
my heart continued its beat
like a rising hope
of new rhythm and old faith,
of olds words from
a new voice,
of new and old and old and new
of now and then,
of me and you,
of maybes and wants
being stated as certainty with clarity.

i shook
as my head meditated
and worked to remember
that moment,
those words,

that sharing of a shaking
of me, of life, of there,
as my heart smiled.

silence

you are too often missing among us. we raise the noise.
we add and add and add more sound to keep you out.

we fail to know we need you. we crave you, but misinterpret
desires,
crafting new trends of sound, volume.

on an elevator, music.

in a vehicle, music.

on an airplane, noise.

in a home, noise.

noise and more noise. sounds and more sounds. high volume
occupying all
we do wherever we go whenever that might be.

morning noise.
noon noise.
evening noise.

sounds shift but rarely depart to leave space for silence.

we must intentionally choose you.
we only hear you, silence, when we
work hard to push away the noise
and aggressively craft noiselessness.

my left hand holds the steering wheel and my right foot guides
the speed and my left foot rests in her place. i force my right hand
to reach forward and turn the radio off. i do not need the songs,
the news, the noise. i need you, silence. you, that often missed
medicine of my rides.

my eyes stare at a device my left hand holds while walking to exercise. but i'm missing the deeper endeavor of placing a phone away, pushing my tasks aside, pausing my hurried mental sprint, and embracing a neighborhood to be seen, a sky to be observed, air to be slowly and deeply breathed, birds' concerts to be heard, and no tasks to be completed.

in a conversation with a friend i can listen. just listen. thinking not of how i'll respond.

at a meal with myself i can just eat, slowly, calmly. just eat. reaching not for a laptop or phone or other device. staring not at a screen.

being. not doing.

nothing. as a needed something.

resting while in a hurry, appreciating while wanting, grasping while unsure:
silent prayer and thought helps me
accomplish those goals
of little cultural importance but
personal need.

i need nothing. no noise. now.
i need you, dear silence.
i need to hear you.
and learn about life
uncontrolled by the noise
that keeps you hidden from us.

God promises a king[21]

king uzziah dies;
isaiah sees God,
is seen by God.

king saul dies;
people see God,
are seen by God.

saul,
once God's man,
death by suicide,
pride the instrument,
sin the murder.

a nation,
needing king, needing God, needing unity,
turns to david.

who is this man after God's heart?
who is this who becomes king
in keeping with the promise of God?

this king, a boy;
watching sheep, faithful at his task;
an ordinary day.

samuel comes bringing a sacrifice and a flask of oil
no one tells the shepherd of the prophet's arrival.
jesse's boys, line up for inspection;
first one, second one.
looking closely at each son
the prophet comes up empty.
no one else except an after-thought

---

21   1 Chronicles 11:1–3

named david.
the boy comes in,
the word comes down,
the oil flows;
a promise given:
God will make you king.

a king today?
now wears a robe?
ascends the throne?
rules the land?
go back to the field, david,
to the school of sheep.

his music beat the demons swarming in saul's head.
his sling dealt the blow that left goliath dead.
his name became the song the people sang in praise.
his battlefield decisions took the center stage.

a king today?
now wears a robe?
ascends the throne?
rules the land?
find a cave, david.
the king you serve now wants you dead.

this king, a fugitive;
running, hiding, remembering the promise.
refusing to take matters into his own hands,
he does not touch the king.

how can you be the king?
you are no son or grandson.
you come from judah.
if a king comes from your tribe,
he would be from caleb's house,
not from jesse's.
the odds are against you.

a slow and sudden God   105

all you have is a cave, a song, and a promise.
is that enough?
oh yes,
if God sent the cave.
if God sang the song.
if God spoke the promise.

saul falls on his sword
and the nation comes to hebron for a king.
for a king.
a king—
for the Lord spoke the promise.

providence always lines up with the promise
when the time arrives.
never before, never after.
never early or late.

the king of sling and song,
the king of caves,
the king of a divided kingdom,
becomes king of a nation now one—
for the Lord spoke the promise.

the God of light and love,
the God of grace and goodness,
is the God of promise.
He speaks and it is so.
proof may be slow,
but His words take on the robe of reality
when He is ready.

the Quiltmaker[22]

He searched for the fragments, the scraps,
the pieces of cloth of little worth;
He found them,
He found me.
with His hands He joined me with others,
threading us together with His intricate love.
He is the Quiltmaker.
once worthless, i am His;
now one of many diverse squares
made one by the Quiltmaker.
together we are lovely.

---

22   1 Corinthians 12:14–27

the center [23]

the woman in the center,
so unlike me,
yet so similar.
my struggles are different,
but i must, nevertheless,
stand with her
surrounded by the stones.
i am sinner.
i have lived the lie.
i have no defense,
only a hope
that the One Who loved her
loves me also.
a hope that i,
though deserving the stones,
will be forgiven.
a hope that this One Who stoops to write in the sand
will stoop to write His love in my life.

---

23   John 8:1–11

the lies we believe

thoughts cascade, crash,
rise again,
lead me on,
drive me, push me,
pull me, lure me;
can this wait?
why now?
all you venomous beasts,
ready yourself for your destruction;
i will not torture you slowly,
as has been your method;
i will swiftly stop your maddening crusade
of lies and condemnation and paranoia,
halting your reign of terror,
stopping you in your hideous tracks,
divorcing you
and embracing my New Lover,
my welcome companion,
my exit from control and compulsion:

Peace.

preying in His Name

explain the unexplainable.
trivialize the mystery.
sell the free gift.
systemize the profound.
photograph the invisible.
complicate the simple.
simplify the complicated.
climb into a ritualistic rut
        and live there forever.
cherish the old wineskins.
patronize your weakness.
turn up the volume to drown out
        the silence.
pick up the pace to dream without
        the sabbath.
institutionalize the capital.
capitalize the institution.
say the name not meant to be spoken.
play the game and spend every token.
memorize it.
mesmerize them.
demand your place by the side.
pull strings,
push straw men,
pray so everyone can hear.
but, don't worry.
it will all be over soon.
very soon.

no excuse[24]

there is none righteous, no not one.
but, there was One righteous, only one.

a Man who came and
told stories about a Kingdom and
opened eyes and
loved people.
He was righteous.

we can try to imitate Him,
but that will not work.
i know,
i tried it.
i never could seem to do it right,
like He did it.

how can we be like Him,
this only One?

i once heard that if we rid our lives
of all our trying
and all our lying,
that in the dying
of this One,
we might find a Treasure.
that the Righteous Man
will spill His blood
and fill our hearts
and kill our flesh.
then tell stories about a Kingdom
and open eyes
and love people
through us.

---

24   Romans 3:1–20

there is none righteous, no not one.
there was One righteous, only one
only in Him
will there ever be others.
only in Him.

the stars; the sand[25]

abraham, see the stars.
abraham, see the grains of sand;
illustrations of the promise I give you.
you are My choice for a father,
a grandfather,
the start of a nation, My nation.
I give you My promise,
like the stars and the sand,
the promise is bigger than you can know,
more than you can count,
taller than your reach,
broader than your vision.
you are the father of so many,
the father of My people.
the first star may be slow in shining,
but the many will come,
will come
from you.
not because you have chosen Me,
but because I have chosen you.

what has happened to that nation,
to that people of promise?
they rejected their Rescuer,
now they stand rejected.
has the promise been forgotten?
nullified by the nation's unbelief?
is the fall permanent, beyond recovery?
no, the promise is permanent.
the unbelief opened the door to a world of nations
to hear and know and see and find and believe.
the hardening of a chosen nation
leads to the softening of all nations

---

25   Romans 11

and allows them to choose.
the cycle will continue,
the belief of the outsiders
provoking jealousy in the insider,
eventually softening the nation now hard.

paul preached to the insiders and outsiders.
the outsiders received him.
He published the results,
hoping to create envy in the hearts
of the star-people, the sand-people,
the sons and daughters of abraham.
God has not forgotten, nor will He ever,
forget the promise,
or the people of promise.
first-fruits offered unto Him
make hallowed the whole.
a holy root transports holy life to the branches.
God, the gardener,
cuts and splices, trims and grafts,
amid a horticulture of surprises.
cutting off natural branches,
grafting wild ones, foreign ones.
why did He choose the natural branches?
grace.
why did He cut them off?
unbelief.
why did He accept the wild branches?
grace.
are they growing now,
so full of life and faith and love and health,
that the discarded branches plead for restoration?
that is the plan.
no place for pride or self-confidence or complacency.
God is merciful and harsh.
God is kind and severe.
God is matchless grace and uncompromising truth.
stern to the disobedient ones.

compassionate to the faithful ones,
if they persevere, walk, stand;
if they continue, follow through, endure.
eternally secure,
but only as the walk remains
inside the boundaries of faith;
then, the marvel of divine grace,
this Master's plan,
astounds again, exceeds expectations,
pushes past the wall of the common
and digs up the promise,
dusts it off,
and revives the dead,
grafts the cut-off branches,
accepts the rejected
who believed their way back into favor,
undeserved,
but reserved for the remnant,
the company of the chosen,
the family of the faith and the faithful:
filled with grace, by God, by grace.
jealous and drawn back,
humble and dependent,
naked and aware;
the other, the holy, the natural and wild.
cloudy? the sun will shine.
dry? the river will run.
lonely? the Father will come.
His plan, His time.
don't worry abraham,
the stars still dot the night sky,
the sand still blankets the desert,
the promise still stands ever firm.
a mighty hand will close the circle,
including you,
and, i pray,
including me.

paul's ambition

paul was convinced,
no doubt;
he knew his purpose, his destiny.
he saw potential in his audience:
full of goodness,
complete in knowledge,
competent to instruct.
what's my excuse?
moses couldn't speak eloquently,
but God called him and used him.
david was forgotten when dad called
in the sons to be anointed king,
but God called him and used him.
isaiah was a man of unclean lips,
but God called him and used him,
jeremiah protested to God:
"i am only a child,"
but God called him and used him.
john the baptist didn't dress right,
rahab was a prostitute,
paul was a killer,
timothy was a kid,
jonah was a wimp;
the list goes on.
anyone can make an excuse
and allow their failures or inexperience or fears
keep them from reaching
their potential in God.
paul would not let the roman christians escape God's plan.
the little jew with a big nose,
scarred face and feeble body,
wrote bold letters and

---

26   Romans 15:14–22

preached long sermons,
traveling fourteen hundred miles
from jerusalem to yugoslavia,
with signs and wonders
following the tracks of his sandaled feet.
he built on no one else's foundation;
he blazed a trail
to reach the lost
and glorify Christ,
in service to God.

so close to a distant world

eyes wide open for a blinding trust;
exploding fragments from the center;
daring strength to stand and enter,
yet, in part, resist the thrust.
clothed for battle, the cause defend;
wings at rest to glide on wind,
ever driven by the flowing
of the surge of a distant world.

twists and turns and trials often;
mountain search for shining gold;
whispers now of tales long told,
when hardness slowly starts to soften.
notice nails and thorns and spear;
open wide for the crystal clear.
trusting eyes now blind but growing
in the sight of a distant world.

overtures that hide their faces;
overriding fact with fiction;
overturning contradiction,
overwhelming empty spaces,
long ago but not so far,
a passing glimpse of a door ajar,
led to love that missed its showing
at the sign of a distant world.

questions

i'm an optimistic realist. i like to take the positive spin on things. but even good lenses don't leave out questions. i've included here studies from scriptural texts which i needed to write as i processed them. the Bible, our emotions, our minds: questions are included in every room in our houses of life. welcome them. ask them. and live, while waiting for answers that might, or might not, come. for me, that's when i write.

have you talked about it?

decades passed. wounds grew deep. relationships were negatively influenced by worries. his mental dialogue replayed: "does what happened to my parents happen to everyone? are all relationships like this? can't love be better?"

initial reluctance to talk was obvious. constant humor played a part of his denial. if relationships became too serious he found an escape.

but he finally talked to a counselor about pains from his past. months of confessions and questions, emotional releases and painful revelations: the therapy was healing him. he learned to identify tendencies. he resisted his reluctance toward relationships. he defeated his patterns of escaping. he learned to love himself, God, and other people.

what thoughts come to you as you read this? if you were speaking to a counselor today, what would you need to discuss? what hurts from your past are controlling your present and future decisions? who should you talk to about it? what's stopping you?

denial. avoidance. escapism. anger. attack. those tendencies are not the medicines we need. seeking the correct help is. facing reality — with the right people traveling with us — can help us transition from the danger of denial toward recovery.

begin. begin soon.

do you see this?

my book list keeps on growing
recommended reading knowing
not everyone will open up a page.
but maybe a few stories
can help them see the glories
and heal some of their deep and inner rage.

my song selection widens
as at times i'm just abiding
during moments in this hurried world called life.
but maybe just a new song
can help this soul along
and bring a little peace amid the strife.

that deeper reality;
oh, do you see this?
that holy mystery;
oh, do you see this?
i hope none of us will miss
the wonder in our midst.
i hope we see this.

my many friends i deeply miss
and my wife's not home for a simple kiss
on a day i seem to need them all so much.
but an inner voice assures me
that the questions will not lure me
away from this One Who'll quietly touch.

that deeper reality;
oh, do you see this?
that holy mystery;
oh, do you see this?
i hope none of us will miss

the wonder in our midst.
i hope we see this.

right now,
He's among us.
right now,
He's within us.
this mystery of grace
looking in our face,
no matter how we feel,
let's believe that He is real
right now.

that deeper reality;
oh, do you see this?
that holy mystery;
oh, do you see this?
i hope none of us will miss
the wonder in our midst.
i hope we see this.

why?[27]

why can't i know that friend's name?
why can't i spell the words that come to my mind?
and, my mind, my mind, will it ever be the same?
the shame i feel leads me
to wonder if we had made a deal
and i failed my portion of the agreement. they've told me before.
so many of them have told me before.
i've told myself before:
don't ask God why.
but why? why can't i ask You why?
You are the One Who Knows.
You are the One Who Cares.
even if You don't answer, maybe
it will help me to ask.
wouldn't it? couldn't it?
Father, may i?
was it my lack of faith that caused a disease?
has sin put me in a spell of waiting
for me to become a better person before being healed?
or am i just one of many people
who hurt, who cry, who fail to recall?
and am i just one of many who needs You, who needs You today?
not Your answers or Your explanations
or Your solutions or Your miracles.
You. just You.
maybe that is the Ultimate Answer
to my unlimited questions.
maybe You are.

---

27   Chris Maxwell, *Changing My Mind* (Franklin Springs, GA: LifeSprings Resources, 2005) 29–30.

so many others live beside me in this new home, this hospital, this center of recovery,
the surgical discovery of life and change and lives so much the same.
they live in rooms on this same floor on this same hall, but who sees them there?
who prays for them?
i wasn't sure about myself;
i felt like a stranger in a world of mystery. but i wasn't alone.
others, those still normal and still themselves, came to see me and to care. but those strangers living in rooms near me in this world?
who has come to care?
who is there to stare?
how can i share my life with the world so nearby?

---

28   Chris Maxwell, *Changing My Mind* (Franklin Springs, GA: LifeSprings Resources, 2005) 33.

who?[29]

---

unique pain to me. not pleasant.
good in the long run? i shall see. He shall see.
my God, that is who.
He can turn the painful into peaceful, pleasant growth.
we doubt it. we struggle to see it.
He can do it.
i prayed with my dear friends
that He would do it for me through
this crazy time. this time
i hated.

---

29   Chris Maxwell, *Changing My Mind* (Franklin Springs, GA:
LifeSprings Resources, 2005) 44.

legalism[30]

welcome to a controlling, legalistic church.
we hope you endure your stay.
the scenery is plastic,
but pleasant and predictable.
the fence on the right will keep you in,
the fence on the left will keep out sin.
we need you and you need us;
come on in without a fuss,
to the world
where we look alike and believe alike,
smile a lot and smile alike.
learn the language and speak it well.
let us make your decision for you:
what to do,
where to go,
what to wear,
how much to know.
we take small children like you by the hand
and request that you leave all valuables behind.
remain still,
and keep your eyes and ears inside our vehicle
at all times.
we hope you endure your stay
in our world,
our black and white world,
our smug world,
our small world
after all.

---

30   Matthew 7:1–5

decision

i've cried and prayed, my mind has strayed;
i sit atop the fence.
i hold on tight and then let go
in constant dissonance.

a fight at bethel, a rainbow painted sky,
a damascus road, an angel's sigh,
a cloud by day, a fire by night.
something loud or something bright,
reduce the risk and rescue me
from tossing to and fro;
this steady agitation;
confusion—where to go.
which job, what spouse, which car, what house;
will no one let me know?
to acquiesce or attack the choice?
against or with the flow?

i will ponder prayerfully
the road which i should take;
then i'll trust my Counselor
Who knows and holds my fate.

wait for the Lord31

wait for the Lord?
that action forms a good beginning.
then, be strong and take heart:
living with power and purity.
wait for the Lord;
that action finds a way to keep us going.
one list of four calls: three commands. the
one listed twice, not by accident.
first and last, beginning and end, starting and finishing:
wait on the Lord, the One worth waiting for.
no, He is not gone.
no, He is not unable.
yet, to us the call stands:
wait on the Lord.
to us, time focuses
eyes and hearts in such a
strong, rough way.
during the delay
we hear the Spirt say:
be strong and take heart.
that is our start.
while we wait
God will not be late.
He knows best, does best,
is best.
wait for Jesus? He has come.
wait for Spirit? He has come.
inside of us, now, it is possible for Him to live.
wait for the Lord.
does He dwell within?
if so, being strong and taking heart become possible.
the Savior's strength in us.

---

31   Psalm 27:14

the Living God, the Loving God,
alive and loving us this day,
as we wait and work,
to Him be glory today and forever,
amen.

seasons

some movements follow traditional themes of the
church calendar. i think that is good. more of us
need to. the structure reminds us. the repetition
reinforces importance of historical realities. these
poems reveal my method of remembering and
bringing the traditions into my everyday life.

my new year's resolution

holding the past,
or being held by it,
can offer a variety of
sufficient excuses.
holding the past,
or being held by it,
can limit vision,
luring decisions toward
unnecessary restrictions.
holding the past,
or being held by it,
can control us.

but facing realities,
though deep and dark,
though bloody and sad,
gives us a chance
to change things,
to change how we
view things,
and to, then,
be changed ourselves.

rather than holding
on to what
holds us back,
let's face the regrets
with the grace of release.
instead of reliving
day by day by day by day,
let's say today
the time is now
for the past chapter to end.
all future chapters can,

and will, be affected by
the previous tension,
but the plot must not be
dependent on those stories
to guide it.
it must now
venture into new land,
new hands,
new hope for new days.

forgiving

forgive us our trespasses,
we pray.
as we forgive those who have trespassed against us,
we say.
a decision we make,
is forgiveness.
not waiting until
a payment is made,
an apology requested,
a confession voiced,
an awareness of wrong.
not waiting at all
but choosing to forgive.
no longer holding an action
against another.
maybe the person needing
to be forgiven has no
knowledge of their need.
maybe they know
but don't care.
maybe they continue
to believe they're right.
forgive anyway.
that's the way
toward healing.

the cost of purity

a month, an april, a pure reminder.
my fingers hit keys to type words in advance,
and what type of day did i begin?
a wednesday,
this one and only wednesday
that will be this way at this time
like this the only now, as is, we shall know.
written on a wednesday, ash wednesday.
the hours that
alert us, remind us, refresh us,
as lent season starts by proclaiming
these fingers typing are lent to me in the now
but will soon return to dust.
from, then back again: ashes to ashes.
so why a peek at ashes to alert us, april?
a change in time?
a day for fools?
a diamond, a daisy,
an uncivil war, a revere ride?
a liner sinking dust into dust on water?
the breaking of a home-run record?
births of writers, warriors, presidents, and pole climbers?
rabbits and eggs and candles and cakes?
for us, now, much more.
the ashes have hope because of
this month's reminders.
a week: holy.
a sunday: palm.
a thursday: maundy.
a friday: good.
a saturday: dark?
a sunday: alive.

this april,
let us remember our ashes,
let us lift our palms,
let us drink and eat,
let us wake and pray,
let us listen to the tearing of temples,
let us remain as fools for the
Dead One Who Now Lives.
breathe with Him now.
Him: risen.
us: receiving and believing.

an april month, reminding us of the cost to be pure
as my fingers hit keys to type words in advance,
as my heart hopes to receive
a washing and a cleansing, and be changed,
not just springing forward in time,
but a new man, washing in a new spring,
made clean
for all time.
a change needed for this fool.
amen.

the night[32]

He walked on the water.
He took the hand of a dead girl and lifted her to life.
He fed thousands,
yet always made time for the few. the people
loved Him and hated Him.
marching through life, propelled by Love, filled with Truth,
radiating Glory,
Jesus edged ever closer to His death
with each holy step.
by caring for sinners and confronting saints
He left detractors little option; they could
erase Him or exalt Him, they could
give their lives to Him or discover a way to take away His.
that night, the drama of His destiny began beating.
loudly. closely.
hearing its relentless cadence, His inner world grew dark;
darker than the unusually dark world around Him on this night.
yes, He was God.
yes, He was man.
He knew of the purpose, of the plan.
yet, He felt.
He felt deeply.
maybe to help relieve His pain,
maybe to help them learn to feel true pain,
He invited His disciples.
so many invitations, but this one was unique.
He called them,
these He had experienced life with for three adventurous years,
He called them to the garden.
deeper into darkness.

---

32   Chris Maxwell, *Pause with Jesus: Encountering His Story in Everyday Life*, (Travelers Rest, SC: True Potential Potential, Inc., 2015) 233–238.

deeper into His pain.

deep in prayer with His Father.

then, He called three to go all the way with Him:

peter. james. john.

He invited them to agony.

not joy.

not to gratification and gain.

to emptiness, to loneliness.

troubled, full of sorrow, He walked.

this God-Man looked, sounded, much more man, much less God.

voicing His pain in candid words,

His honesty kicked all pretensions aside,

admitting sorrow, deathlike sorrow, overwhelmed Him.

He invited three to stay with Him,

speaking like a needy man, rather than a needed man.

they were to keep watch, to remain alert, to give Him that moment.

He went farther into the dark heart of gethsemane and

fell face first in desperation. He cried to Father

and asked for reprieve: "maybe there is another way.

must I drink of the bitter cup?" the words carried

His brokenness, His turmoil; they proved His pathos.

Jesus did not stop with His desire; He refused to conclude

after sobbing out His hope for an alternative.

"no matter, God, I will do as You see fit.

carry out Your plan." He rose from prayer, from blood, from sweat,

and returned to His watchmen.

He had given them a privileged charge.

He found them sleeping.

He called them.

He coddled them, taught them, trained them.

then He needed them in a different way

but they slept.

to peter, who was out like a rock,

He offered a rebuke tempered only

by His exhaustion. "an hour isn't so much, is it? only one hour and

you cannot watch with Me, watch for Me?

temptation will rob you unless you learn

to watch and pray.
the battle rages;
flesh so weak and spirit strong.
feed your spirit. do not satisfy the flesh."
a second time He cried to God in prayer.
speaking the same words.
a second time He returned.
a second time He found His closest friends sleeping.
a third time He cried to God in prayer.
speaking the same words.
a third time He returned.
a third time He found His closest friends sleeping.
how sad. their sleepy refusal to spend the night in prayer
when the Master solicited their participation.
didn't they sense His hurt? didn't they?
they didn't fight off sleep to embrace prayer, to share pain. was it
could not or would not?
am i different?
what replaces my prayer as sleep did theirs?
Jesus invited them to pray in the dark.
they slept.
they never liked His talk of death anyway.
maybe a restless nap helped them escape
the nagging awareness that He really was going away soon.

years have passed since that dark night.
maybe He weeps even now at God's right hand.
no tears in heaven? can He see
the child slapped by an impatient parent,
the man battling an incurable disease,
the family on the brink of collapse,
the killing of the innocent,
the laughter of the guilty,
the multitudes unmoved by His love? can He see?
if He sees, He cries.
if He cries, He prays.
always interceding.

if He sees and cries and prays,
He calls us. He invites us
into the darkness of the garden.
spend the night with Him
in crucial prayer.
not pleading for trinkets or hoping for fun.
now, crying for Life and dying for Love.
tonight, with the drum of destiny
beating, beating, beating,
close and clear,
can we watch one hour?
a bitter cup and a Father's will,
temptation and tears, flesh and spirit.
at this time He cries out to God in prayer.
at some time He will return.
will He find us sleeping?

good friday

the rain is falling hard, though beginning to slow:
wind, thunder, and lightning started my day.

sounds and sights:
clouds covering the light
from a morning sun shining our way
and birds sing as if they are expecting a nice day.

the storm reminds me of
dangers, of
change, of
wind blowing our way,
or winds blowing us away and away and away and away.

redundancy of rituals can serve only as routine reminders of
life stories from historical events
and ancient traditions.
or they can help us revisit,
help us remember and reflect.
inspire us to review their original occurrences
for more than knowing about or recalling.
but to receive. to be renewed.

i contemplate and journal
a free verse version of
verses of freedom which
biblically, historically, and personally
invade my stormy, rainy friday
and remind me why we title this day of
crucifixion, of
death, of
blood, of
good friday, of
why we call this friday *good*.

the drama of the resurrection

King Jesus.
so many prophecies trumpeting His majestic coming,
anticipated,
long awaited,
born in seclusion,
in a feeding trough;
no room in the inn.
the prophecies continued:
He will cause rising,
He will cause falling.
pushing but not too hard;
proving but not for Himself,
all for the Father.
they loved Him and they hated Him,
they listened and they shut their ears.
He never stopped loving;
an unusual love filled with Truth
minus trappings and pretense;
He healed, raised, taught, disciplined, wept.

King Jesus.
the coronation was almost embarrassing:
riding a colt on a carpet of cloaks;
they hailed Him,
cheers and branches highlighting a poor-man's parade.
He ate with His closest companions
and showed them again
what it meant to be a King.
His scepter?
a towel.
the road to glory?
humble service.

King Jesus.
then came the garden;
those He served
did not serve Him.
they slept.
He prayed and cried and bled.
judas kissed Him.
soldiers beat Him.
crowds sentenced Him.
friends left Him.
pilate washed hands.
a rooster crowed.

King Jesus.
carried a crossbeam through the city.
they lifted Him high
in crucified agony,
He died on the town garbage heap
nailed to the tree.

King Jesus.
sunday morning,
early morning,
the ladies who loved Him
went to the tomb to anoint His body
wondering all the way:
how could they roll the stone?
but the stone was moved.
an angel sat nearby
and asked them:
"why do you seek the Live One in a place of death?
He is not here,
He is risen,
just as He promised."

King Jesus.
the ladies rejoiced
and the disciples doubted,
but peter ran to the tomb.
there was no body there,
only strips of linen undisturbed.
he went away
wondering all the way
what could this mean?

King Jesus.

the solution

the plot unfolded perfectly.
meeting Light on the battlefield of earth,
> dark fought hard.
crowds jeered, friends fled, pilate washed his hands.
people—pawns—carried out dark's disgusting plans.
a whip ripped open an Innocent Man's back,
a midday sky turned to a sad shade of black
as a painful death visited the Unusual One
> Who claimed to be Divine.
jubilant demon hordes screamed in pleasure
> as they scampered unseen in the atmosphere
> above a world they now would rule.
the One Who could stop them didn't.
the One Who seemed more powerful wasn't.
His body hung limp and lifeless,
nailed to the killing-tree
planted on a mound
for all to see.
the fiendish spirits did not know the sudden twist
> the story was about to take.
the religious rulers did not expect this end
> to be the beginning.
the solemn empty tomb held the body like a womb;
then, in a flash of light, a birth:
from death to life.
Messiah made a move His enemies did not foresee.
Messiah made a move His enemies could not counter.
victory of Love, defeat for hate.
death died and Life lived again.
Savior divided man and guilt,
> multiplied hope,
> subtracted sin,
> added meaning and purpose.

Savior solved the problem
of death, of life, of today, of tomorrow;
my problem
solved
by God.

national tragedies

national tragedies, alarms,
wake nations from the sleep of the routine,
bring out the worst, the best,
distrust and trust,
unite a people so usually separate.

president kennedy,
killed in dallas,
a world left wondering why,
honoring him,
remembering where they were at that moment,
dreaming of what could have been.
to carry on, but never to forget.

space shuttle challenger,
explodes in the sky
and paints the grim picture
of its demise,
a haunting cloud,
for all to see
and none to escape.

single topic of conversation.
only prayer on lips.
cause of tears freely flowing.
the nation:
wondering, honoring, remembering, dreaming;
carrying on, but never forgetting.

against all hope, abraham believed[33]

a snow storm in orlando.
a world without war.
a car that never breaks down.
impossibilities? certainly.
some impossibilities happen:
communism outlawed in the soviet union;
a crumbling wall in germany;
the braves in the series.
but, few impossibilities
could be more impossible than
decorating the nursing home
for a baby shower.
blue balloons to celebrate the birth of isaac
a bundle of impossibility
God placed in the hands
of abraham and sarah
long after their baby-having days had ended.

how could it happen?
because God said it would.
abraham ignored the evidence
strongly stacked against the promise.
he believed.
he compared the odds to God.
no contest.

faith is believing,
and accepting,
and trusting,
and depending,
not just mental,

---

33   Romans 4

it changes all of life,
and challenged all lies.

what about works?
abraham's deeds were important,
but they grew out of his faith;
they did not produce his faith.
a worker earns wages,
a believer receives a gift.
the difference is great.

what about forgiveness?
david loved God, yet he sinned.
facing his sin,
he felt hopeless.
unable to earn forgiveness,
the singing shepherd-king threw himself
at the mercy of the sinless Shepherd-King.
he had faith.
he was forgiven.

what about righteousness?
can a man live right on his own power?
no, neither a good man or bad.
neither a religious man or pagan.
righteousness is a five-letter word: faith.
God places a check in the righteousness column
beside the name of the one who
believes, accepts, trusts, and depends.
He credits the account.

what about grace?
we sing about how amazing it is,
but attempt to amaze God,
and others,
and ourselves,
by working our way to righteousness.

by grace through faith:
the equation of salvation.
a free gift.
undeserved favor.
love for hate.
life for death.
a walk through the door of faith
provides entrance into the
enchanted land of grace.

what about hope?
abraham hoped when all hope was gone.
he saw a light in the darkness.
he drank from an oasis in the desert.
he ate a feast in a time of famine.
faith, hope, and love:
the most forgotten of these is hope.
the man of faith is a man of hope,
believing in a God

Who creates *ex nihilo*;
something from nothing,
yes from no,
sun through the clouds.
keep believing because
the boy slays the giant,
the spies escape unharmed,
the tomb turns up empty,
the sky rips open with a shout,
the tears are dried forever.

what about justification?
how can a sinner no longer be a sinner?
how can the God Who hates sin
rescue the wicked from the waters of evil?
He extends His arms
in an act of grace.

the sinner who reaches back in an act of faith
will be ushered to safety.
the sinner can then face God
as if he had never sinned.
faith unto salvation.
all because of grace.
what a plan.
what a God.

peace with God³⁴

adam, lost in the garden.
a high priest alone into the Holy of Holies.
a veil: separation and distance.
man.   God.
distant, and at war.

but, paul announces peace.
from enmity to friendship.
the reason for the peace?
justification through faith.
the result of the peace?
access to the grace of God.
what to do now, but rejoice in the peace?
now we have hope, hope in glory, God's glory.
no longer under the wrath.
the death sentence served by an Innocent Man.
alienated no longer,
in a place of high favor with God,
we celebrate the hope of glory.

our past? forgiven.
our present? favored.
our future? perfect.

Jesus, cursed on the tree.
a common man walks with many into God's Presence.
a veil: torn apart.
man and God.
together, and at peace.

---

34   Romans 5:1–2

death and life: from adam to Christ[35]

one man can change the future.
one thought, one decision, one act.
i am here because many individuals
changed the world
through their thoughts, decisions, actions.
david repented and asked for mercy.
augustine used his intellect to search out the riches of God.
martin had the courage to post his objections.
the wesleys rode countless miles,
john preaching, charles composing;
establishing new methods of evangelism and discipleship.
c.s. lewis wrote it.
keith green sang it.
a mother. a teacher. a pastor. a friend. a stranger.
an individual can influence the world.

adam did.
his thought, his decision, his action.
no fruit could have tasted so delightful
that poisoning the human race did not matter.
the reign of sin and the reign of death.
one man's disobedience.
all become sinners.
his name? "mankind."
and his behavior influenced all under that name.
law was given after the fact of sin
to reveal the principle at work in the world.
judgment and condemnation.
separation from God.
degeneration and decay.
death through the disobedience of one.

---

35   Romans 5:12–21

Christ did.
His thoughts, decisions, actions were unto the Father.
the agonizing pain of the cruel cross was worth it
to work the pardon of the human race.
the reign of grace and life.
one Man's obedience, even to the death.
all may become righteous.
His name? "Anointed One."
and His love was proof of that sacred title.
paying the penalty, moving men from guilt to grace.
abolishing the principle at work in the world.
gift and justification.
communion with God.
regeneration and delight.
life through the obedience unto death of One.

what about me?
will i choose sin or grace?
death or life?
stay in adam and die separated from God
or abide in Christ and live in fellowship with God?
i must remember His death and receive His life.

i take the bread.
i look at it.
i think, i decide, i act.
in need of mercy, desperate for life,
i partake,
and swallow the death that brings a resurrection.

i take the cup.
i consider the cross.
thinking, deciding, acting;
because i am so thirsty for forgiveness,
i drink,
and swallow the life-flow that brings a transformation.

i remember His death and receive His life.
in Him i live and move and have my being.
in Him i am justified.
i live.
now, as i live,
i think, i decide, i act.
this man's obedience through Christ
will change the world,
for today,
for tomorrow,
for Him.

thanksgiving then and now

many thanksgivings ago
i toured brief rides with my parents and sisters
through a small town
to meet a large family
to eat large meals
on a holiday of georgia's november
weather with
football indoors and
football outdoors and
football opinions while
enjoying the discussions of memories
and the creations of memories,
as more memories were in the process of
crafting and designing.
the smells of turkey and desserts, of bread and tea.
the cool georgia air and warm family hearts.
the smiles.
the conversations.
memoirs discussed:
those days, those times, those ways, those stories,
those songs, those wounds,
those questions,
those opinions,
those decisions.
those, these, then, us.
there, then, here, now.
relatives eating and chatting
relative issues, or issues assumed
to be such but proven otherwise during dialogue,
which was okay because in some cases
conversations themselves were worth the words
and smiles and disagreements and laughter
and amount of calories enjoyed for thanksgiving.

many thanksgivings ago
i drove with my wife, debbie, and sons from florida to georgia
year after year
for a week of giving thanks and receiving food,
and giving and receiving
christmas presents as our one-month-early-because-we-are-together-
now
holiday celebration.
the drives, the music, the conversations.
the gatherings, the gifts,
the good times had by all.
debbie's fall underground,
pain still felt decades later,
a story still being told.
ball games played together.
ball games watched together.
injuries, laughter,
feasting, singing,
pain, pleasure.
stories from then still being told.
life.
death.
a mama so distant
for too long;
a story remembered, honored,
and still being told.
memories and pictures and
more meals and more conversations,
more stories
still being told.
of history. of hope.
of then and now.
of is and isn't.
of us and them.
of life and death.
of vehicles breaking down and
brains breaking down and

relationships breaking down,
but Jesus somehow meeting us in those places
of broken days and broken lives and broken families.
eat, and be still.
love, and be still.
remember, if you can,
and be still.

a thanksgiving like this one, on these days.
life, again, though different, in northeast georgia,
living, again, where i never expected to return,
and seeing seasons and their colors beside me,
and feeling seasons and their temperatures beside me,
as i type with chilled fingers and smile with a face
of true joy and glance at a rabbit toward the east
and a chipmunk having what resembles
a panic attack toward the west.
i guess we can call this life.
in a fallen world, yes, we can call it life.
but this is, as i may say too often, a world of wonder.

i give thanks.
of family before me.
of family beside me.
of wife and sons, of their spouses and their children.
of father and sisters and friends and strangers.
of that mama so distant and close
on a thanksgiving week for meals and memories
and mysteries,
and me remembering again that this moment
is of value,
that all people are of value,
that i am to be thankful
as i love those who hate,
as i forgive those who view their lives
as having done no wrong,
as i realized my

damaged brain and damaged life and damaged everything
is not everything.
there is more.
it is near.
i smile.
i eat.
and i give thanks.

christmas[36]

i am an infant,
crawling around on the floor.
staring up at the stairway,
i long to rise;
stand, walk, run, climb,
ascend to the top
and meet God.
but i am a baby,
incapable of such a feat.

God is there.
i am here.

the ten steps,[37]
stone stairs that offer access to God
are too formidable;
i am too weak, too immature.
God speaks from the majestic height:
He has heard my cries.
He sends a Rescuer
Who descends the stairs,
a Giant shrinking in size
as He nears the bottom.
i am shocked, stunned.
when He arrives at the floor
He is an infant
crawling with me.

He has become like me.
but how will we climb the steps

---

36   Luke 2:1–7; Chris Maxwell and Mary DeMent, *Unwrapping His Presence: What We Really Need for Christmas* (Oviedo, FL: Higher Life Development Services, Inc., 2010) 6–8.
37   The Ten Commandments, Exodus 20:1–17

and arrive at the place of our longing?
somehow this Babe lifts me up.
one step. then two. then another.
pushing and straining;
i see what is happening:
He is slowly dying,
exhausting His energy
by powering me to the top.

i arrive at God's presence
full of sadness and joy; i sing for me and hurt for the Rescuer.

i see God.
i see God.

i think i know Him.
i think He knows me.

He smiles.
i cry.
His smile looks similar to a Baby's.
my cry is now the cry of a man.

the paper protected the present.
it also presented the gift as something it wasn't.
colors, images.
a cover, a mask.
though lovely and friendly,
the imagery lies about reality.
paper, protecting and promoting a fictional fix,
cast in a mix of amazement, does its task of deception.
is it something i want,
or something i wait for?
is it someone i am,
or someone i long to become?
don't the gifts give way
on a holiday?
aren't they torn opened
to trash the covers aside?
they are because
what is inside matters.
what paper protects
our presence?
why do i pretend, presenting
me as someone i'm not?
i must remove the
colors, images.
i must rip
my cover, my mask.
i'll give the Worker the task
of tearing, opening, trashing
that old me away,
and convincing me
this christmas:
what is inside is
what matters.

---

38   Chris Maxwell and Mary DeMent, *Unwrapping His Presence: What We Really Need for Christmas* (Oviedo, FL: Higher Life Development Services, Inc., 2010) 86–87.

praying as years go by

a decade travels, comes and goes,
no one knows this start to finish
as well as expected when dreams began
in the beginning.

during these ten years i have pastored,
learning and listening and loving as i go,
i have pastored a people i love.

i am not good enough, i know;
my God must guide me, i know,
for this role to continue, for this goal to come near me.
my God must show His power every hour
coming among us to see us through.
of my three children, one has exceeded ten,
one is close to ten, and one has years until then.
as a pastor, ten years have passed with
promises, pressure, pleasure;
with hopes and dreams, as we seek to live as a holy team:
God's children together with love and life.

days plus days equal a decade. friends plus friends equal a family.
Spirit plus Scripture equals hope for help in this life,
in this place, at this time, among this church.

we can live with God in us. we can live.
we can love with God among us. we can love.
forgiven ones can forgive those who hurt them.
dreams come true through prayers and praise.
worship rises, sermons send lessons, relationships remain.

i remember the beginning. i reach into the present,
aware that God's power must see us
and see us through.
i pray that He does.

please pray that He does,
that these ten years,
that the next two months.
that today,
He will empower us to live for His glory and our good.
another day, and old and new way, no delay:
stay surrendered to God, serving one another,
during the quick trip of traveling time,
remain in the God Who remains in His children.

dancing out of death

a mystery marches across time.
man, in cadence matching the beat of this world.
God, His steps dancing to a different rhythm.
man moves to the usual; God to the unusual.
questions asked by the man, and the life pursued
with selfish motives and uncommon vigor.
answers given by God, and life offered
in strange manifestations of uncommon valor:
a Babe, crying in a manger.
a Child, astonishing the scholars.
a Teacher, forgiving sins and opening eyes.
a Man claiming to be God.
could it be?
a Man in step with the song of heaven, seeking men
to join Him
in the dance of difference?
could it be?
a celebration of joy that ends abruptly one day
as the music stops
and the sky grows black
and the clouds roll in.
the end? or an interlude in a longer song?
then . . . drums! shouts! trumpets! singing!
the beat begins anew,
more energy and purpose,
moving   like   never   before,
this dance from death to Life.
darkness retreats and Light shines.
the Song invites us to step in,
to take the scarred hand of the Dancer and move
like never before
across time with God.

epilogue: forty miles

pages of poetry conclude,
not as a wall built but as a world of words
beginning again, just unseen for now.
your words and my words,
words written and read and interpreted
and written again and interpreted again.
poems of stories told, felt, assumed.
poems of dreams waiting to come true.

please pursue those dreams.
those vague, covered by the clouds,
what-will-this-possibly-become dreams,
carefully and courageously
pursue them.

like a brief ride through roads known well,
though, this time, under construction,
surprised by traffic, surprised by speed,
surprised by weather, surprised by self,

cherish every mile.
intentionally smile, letting now
be forty seconds of value, letting now
be forty minutes of peace, letting now
be a forty mile ride of joy, letting now
be new for you.

as you think of forty days from today,
don't miss the forty wonders of today.
breathe them in. each one. slowly.
now is this now.
here is right here.

glance back into this collection
of my own confessions.
contemplate on your own.

simplify it all.
summarize in forty words your own
why me
and your own
why this
and your own
what now
and your own
what next.

and become a poetic reality
with forty miles of words,
of thoughts, of prayers,
realizing your life
is, moment by moment,
important and valuable and
painful and frightening and
the poems of your life
are being crafted now.
let them be.

help them be.
through effort and little effort,
through hard work and deep sleep,
through writing and editing,
through watching miles pass by,
try now to believe
your life poem is important.

so conclude with a start, a ride, an adventure.
go knowing and not knowing,
go now, embracing forty miles of words.

About Chris Maxwell

Chris Maxwell is a husband, father, and grandfather. He is a writer, spiritual life director, international speaker, and a man who loves people. Chris hopes to be a voice of encouragement through words spoken, words written, and a life lived.

Website/ Blog: www.chrismaxwell.me

Twitter: @CMaxMan

Facebook: Facebook.com/PausewithChrisMaxwell

Email: CMaxMan11@ gmail.com

Other Books by Chris Maxwell

Beggars Can Be Chosen: An Inspirational Journey Through the Invitations of Jesus

Changing My Mind: A Journey of Disability and Joy

Unwrapping His Presence: What We Really Need for Christmas

Pause: The Secret to a Better Life, One Word at a Time

Pause for Moms: Finding Rest in a Too Busy World

Pause for Pastors: Finding Still Waters in the Storm of Ministry

Pause with Jesus: Encountering His Story in Everyday Life

Underwater: When Encephalitis, Brain Injury, and Epilepsy Change Everything